It's Not Complicated—errata

Creamy Spinach Artichoke Pasta
page 78

The following paragraph is missing from the method, following "...of the pasta water":

Combine the oil and garlic in a large ovenproof skillet over medium heat. Sauté for 1 minute. Add the crushed red pepper, then the spinach and artichokes. Sauté for a couple of minutes, then season with the basil and salt and pepper. Stir in ¾ cup (180 ml) of the reserved pasta water. Stir in the cream cheese until it melts. Add the pasta and ½ cup (120 ml) of the pasta water to the pan. Toss to combine. If the pasta looks too dry, add more pasta water. Remove from the heat and stir in the Parmesan. Top with the mozzarella and broil for 2 to 3 minutes, until bubbly and golden brown. Serve hot.

IT'S NOT COMPLICATED

IT'S NOT COMPLICATED

Simple Recipes for Every Day

Katie Lee Biegel

PHOTOGRAPHY BY LUCY SCHAEFFER

ABRAMS, NEW YORK

FOR RYAN. *A lifetime of memorable meals with our family is to come.*

CONTENTS

Introduction

6

CHAPTER ONE

COCKTAILS
AND
NIBBLES

8

CHAPTER TWO

SALADS
AND
SOUPS

38

CHAPTER THREE

ENTRÉES

76

CHAPTER FOUR

SIDES

140

CHAPTER FIVE

DESSERTS

166

CHAPTER SIX

BREAKFASTS
AND
BRUNCHES

192

Acknowledgments

216

Index

217

The title of this cookbook is a nod to one of my favorite films, *It's Complicated*, by my all-time favorite director, Nancy Meyers. The worlds that she creates in her movies are comforting in every sense. Her set design alone is a feast for the eyes—soothing shades of neutrals and whites, crisp-clean kitchens, effortless-looking dinner tables filled with platters of food. I always say I wish I could live in one of her movies. (Hence me in a cream turtleneck à la Diane Keaton in *Something's Gotta Give*, making spaghetti with clams, in a beach house in the Hamptons.)

Since real life is a lot messier, especially given the state of the world, I try to focus on the good stuff, which is generally the least complicated: My month-old daughter's chunky cheeks, the fall air, walks with our little dog, Gus, a new season of *The Bachelor*, and a really good meal with my husband.

Food is how I like to show love, how I take care of people, and how I can make my small corner of the world into a warm, comforting space. To me, there is nothing better than a perfectly roasted chicken, a steak simply seasoned with coarse salt and pepper, or a chocolate chip cookie, hot out of the oven. These recipes are not the trendiest or the most Instagram-ready, but they are truly my favorites, the simple ones I turn to over and over, and the ones I hope will become your own.

Much love,

Katie Lee Biegel

October 9, 2020

Tequila
and Tonic

12

Amalfi Spritz

12

Lillet Fizz

13

Iced Peach Bourbon
Lemonade Tea

13

Cosmo Americano

16

Mango
Mexican Mule

16

Sgroppino

17

Tomato
Bruschetta

18

Lemon Caper
Deviled Eggs

20

Water Chestnuts
Wrapped
in Bacon

21

Crab Toast

23

Pumpkin Hummus

24

Fig and Pepita
Goat Cheese Log

25

Celery with
Cream Cheese
and
Everything Bagel
Seasoning

26

Blue Cheese–
Stuffed Dates

28

Prosciutto Crisps

28

Crispy Artichoke
Hearts

29

Herbed Cheese
with Crostini and
Radishes

32

Hot Roasted
Eggplant Dip

34

Bloody Mary
Shrimp Cocktail
"Ceviche"
with
Plantain Chips

35

chapter one

———

COCKTAILS AND NIBBLES

Tequila and Tonic

I haven't really been a gin drinker since I was in college (may or may not have had too much one night), but one of Ryan's favorite drinks is the gin and tonic. I just can't do it, so when he gets out the tonic, I use silver tequila instead of gin. I really like the tequila with the bitter flavor of the tonic, and the lime just makes me think margarita (which is my number-one drink).

2 ounces (60 ml) chilled silver tequila

3 ounces (90 ml) chilled tonic water

Lime slices

Fill a rocks glass with ice. Add the tequila and tonic and stir. Garnish with the lime slices and serve immediately.

YIELD
1 serving

TOTAL TIME
5 minutes

Amalfi Spritz

I have a deep affinity for the Amalfi Coast. It's heaven on earth, as far as I'm concerned. My drink of choice is usually an Aperol Spritz, but a few summers ago, while on an excursion to Ravello, I had a spritz made of elderflower liqueur, prosecco, and seltzer. It was garnished with edible flowers, and lemon and cucumber slices. It was almost too pretty to drink. Almost.

1 ounce (30 ml) elderflower liqueur, such as St-Germain

3 ounces (90 ml) prosecco

2 ounces (60 ml) seltzer

Lemon slice

Cucumber slice

Fresh mint sprig

Edible flowers

Fill a wineglass with ice. Pour the liqueur over the ice, then top with the prosecco and seltzer. Serve with a slice of lemon, a slice of cucumber, a sprig of mint, and a sprinkling of edible flowers.

YIELD
1 serving

TOTAL TIME
5 minutes

Lillet Fizz

Cool off on a warm summer evening with this Lillet fizz. I first had Lillet when a friend introduced me to it and I immediately bought several bottles of the fruity, slightly sweet, citrusy French apéritif. It can be used in cocktails but I really like it just with seltzer. I use frozen grapes instead of ice so that it doesn't get diluted and it's a bit more festive.

2 ounces (60 ml) Lillet, chilled

2 ounces (60 ml) seltzer, chilled

5 or 6 frozen grapes

Pour the Lillet and seltzer into a chilled wineglass. Add the frozen grapes. Serve immediately.

YIELD
1 serving

TOTAL TIME
5 minutes

Iced Peach Bourbon Lemonade Tea

Ryan and I spent the first year of our marriage living in Santa Monica. In the nearby neighborhood of Pacific Palisades, a new movie theater opened—and let me tell you, it was *fancy*. You could hit a button at your seat and a server came with all sorts of food and beverage options. When my dad came to visit, we took him to see *Captain America*. He ordered a peach bourbon lemonade and it was dee-lic-ious. We went home and got to mixing up our own version. It's a warm-weather staple at our house now.

6 black tea bags

1 cup (200 g) sugar

4 cups (215 g) ice

2 cups (480 ml) lemonade

1 cup (240 ml) bourbon

½ cup (120 ml) peach schnapps

Peach slices

Fresh mint sprigs

Bring 4 cups (960 ml) water to a simmer over high heat. Turn off the heat and add the tea bags. Let steep for 3 to 5 minutes. Remove the tea bags and stir the sugar into the hot tea until it is dissolved. Pour the warm tea into a pitcher filled with the ice. Stir until the tea is cooled and the ice is melted. Add the lemonade, bourbon, and schnapps. Stir and pour over ice to serve and garnish each drink with peach slices and a sprig of fresh mint.

YIELD
4 to 6 servings

TOTAL TIME
10 minutes

Fig and Pepita
Goat Cheese
Log, page 25

Sgroppino,
page 17

Prosciutto Crisps, page 28

Lillet Fizz,
page 13

Amalfi Spritz,
page 12

Crab Toast,
page 23

Cosmo Americano

When is the last time you had a Cosmo? Has it been a while? I'll forever associate that drink with *Sex and the City*. I'm all for putting a spin on a classic and I am really into bitters at the moment. If you haven't tried Cocchi Americano, I suggest picking up a bottle. It's both sweet and bitter, citrusy, with a touch of spice. You can use it to make a spritz, or try adding an ounce to a Cosmo to get all of your guests asking, "Why is this *so good*?"

- 2 ounces (60 ml) vodka
- 1 ounce (30 ml) cranberry juice
- 1 ounce (30 ml) fresh lime juice
- 1 ounce (30 ml) Cocchi Americano
- Lime twist or wedge

Pour the vodka, cranberry juice, lime juice, and Cocchi Americano into a cocktail shaker filled with ice. Shake vigorously. Pour into a martini glass. Serve with a lime twist or wedge.

YIELD
1 serving

TOTAL TIME
5 minutes

Mango Mexican Mule

Give me a tequila drink and I'm happy. Make it a fruity frozen tequila drink, and I'm over the moon. This is a really fun twist on a Moscow Mule; the sweet mango plays really nicely with the spicy ginger beer. You can absolutely mix up the alcohol, though: If you want to go classic mule, use vodka, or if you want to stay on the Mexican route and make it a little smoky, try mezcal.

- 4 ounces (120 ml) silver tequila
- 2 ounces (60 ml) fresh lime juice
- 1 cup (165 g) frozen mango
- One 12-ounce (360 ml) bottle ginger beer

Put the tequila, lime juice, and mango in a blender. Blend until very smooth. Divide the mixture among four glasses (or copper mugs, if available!). Fill the glasses with ice, then top off each glass with ginger beer.

YIELD
4 servings

TOTAL TIME
5 minutes

Sgroppino

We served sgroppinos at our wedding after dinner as people made their way to the dance floor. It was the perfect refresher after a heavy meal, with the bright lemon flavor to cleanse the palate, vodka to get the party going, and bubbles to make it festive. I warn you, the alcohol is very hard to taste in these, so be careful!

1 small scoop lemon sorbet (about 2 tablespoons)

1 ounce (30 ml) vodka

Prosecco

Fresh mint leaf

Lemon slice

Put the sorbet in the bottom of a champagne flute or coup glass. Top with the vodka and fill the glass with prosecco. Garnish with a mint leaf and slice of lemon.

YIELD
1 serving

TOTAL TIME
5 minutes

Tomato Bruschetta

YIELD

4 servings

ACTIVE TIME

10 minutes

My favorite farm stand, the Green Thumb, grows the most incredibly sweet cherry and grape tomatoes. They have both red and yellow varieties, as well as heirlooms. The tomatoes are so sweet they taste like candy. Is there anything better? I don't think so. I keep this bruschetta recipe quite simple because I just want to taste those tomatoes, so they are only highlighted by good olive oil and salt and pepper, but you can always jazz them up with some fresh basil or even mint.

2 tablespoons extra-virgin olive oil

½ baguette, cut into ¼-inch (6 mm) slices

Kosher salt

1 cup (145 g) cherry or grape tomatoes, cut into quarters

Freshly ground black pepper

Heat a cast-iron skillet over medium-high heat. Add 1 tablespoon oil to the pan and swirl it around to coat. Working in batches if necessary, place the baguette slices in the pan in a single layer. Cook on one side until toasted to golden brown, 2 to 3 minutes. Remove to a serving platter and season with salt.

In a small bowl, combine tomatoes and 1 tablespoon remaining oil. Season to taste with salt and pepper. Spoon tomatoes on top of toast slices and serve.

Lemon Caper Deviled Eggs

I love deviled eggs. *Love.* I always say, "It's not a party at my house without deviled eggs." It's hard to beat the classic rendition, but every now and then I'll mix things up. I came up with this recipe for a dinner I cooked at the South Beach Wine and Food Festival and I topped them with fried oysters. They're obviously delicious that way (anything fried, am I right?), but I like them just as well without the garnish. I've made them with lemon and capers so many times now, I have almost forgotten what they taste like plain!

YIELD
24 deviled eggs

ACTIVE TIME
20 minutes

TOTAL TIME
30 minutes

12 large eggs

1 cup (240 ml) mayonnaise

1 tablespoon yellow mustard

2 teaspoons capers, rinsed and drained

1 small clove garlic, grated

Zest of 1 lemon

Kosher salt and freshly ground black pepper

Fill a large saucepan with water and bring to a boil over high heat. With a ladle, slowly lower the eggs into the water, one by one. Reduce the heat to a low boil and cook for 10 minutes. Drain. When cool enough to handle, peel the eggs.

Slice each egg in half lengthwise. Remove the yolks and place them in a food processor. Arrange the whites, cut side up, on a serving platter. To the food processor, add the mayo, mustard, capers, garlic, lemon zest, ¼ teaspoon salt, and ¼ teaspoon pepper. Process until well blended and smooth, then transfer to a resealable plastic bag. With scissors, snip off a bottom corner from the bag. Using the bag like a pastry bag, pipe the egg yolk mixture into the egg whites. Serve immediately, or store egg whites and yolk mixture separately in the fridge, for one to two days, until ready to fill and serve.

Water Chestnuts Wrapped in Bacon

This is Ryan's signature cocktail-hour snack. He used to only make them at Christmas, but I have talked him into making them all year long. I am a ketchup fanatic and the way it caramelizes when baked on the bacon reminds me of the same effect it has on a meatloaf. Be forewarned, you will want to eat these as soon as they come out of the oven, but let them cool for a minute because they are molten hot!

YIELD
4 to 6 servings

TOTAL TIME
30 minutes

8 slices bacon

One 8-ounce (226 g) can whole water chestnuts

¼ cup (60 ml) ketchup

1 tablespoon brown sugar

½ teaspoon sambal

2 dashes Worcestershire sauce

Toothpicks

Preheat the oven to 425°F (220°C). Line a rimmed baking sheet with parchment paper.

Cut the bacon slices in half or thirds, depending on the type of bacon you are using. Wrap a piece of bacon around each water chestnut and secure with a toothpick. Mix the ketchup, brown sugar, sambal, and Worcestershire sauce in a bowl. Brush each wrapped water chestnut all over with sauce and place on the prepared baking sheet. Bake for 20 to 25 minutes, until the bacon is crispy and the sauce is deep brown. Let cool for 2 to 3 minutes, then serve warm.

Crab Toast

YIELD
4 to 6 servings

TOTAL TIME
10 minutes

This crab toast is our Christmas Eve tradition. It started the first time Ryan and I spent the holiday together. It was just the two of us and we did an all seafood night, starting with this crab toast, then baked stuffed lobsters and plenty of champagne.

1 baguette, cut into ¼-inch (6 mm) rounds

2 tablespoons extra-virgin olive oil

1 small clove garlic, grated

¼ cup (60 ml) mayonnaise

Zest of 1 lemon

Juice of ½ lemon

1 tablespoon minced fresh parsley

3 basil leaves, cut into chiffonade

½ Fresno chile, seeded and minced

⅛ teaspoon kosher salt

Pinch of cracked black pepper

8 ounces (225 g) jumbo lump crabmeat, picked for shells

Preheat the oven to 425°F (220°C). Brush the baguette slices with the oil and toast in the oven for 5 to 10 minutes, or until golden brown. Set aside to cool.

In a bowl, mix the garlic, mayonnaise, lemon zest, lemon juice, parsley, basil, and chile together until fully combined. Season with the salt and pepper. Fold in the crab, making sure not to break up too many clumps. Top each toast with crab mixture (or refrigerate the crab and assemble when ready to serve). Serve immediately.

Pumpkin Hummus

YIELD
4 to 6 servings

TOTAL TIME
5 minutes

I'm a fan of just about anything pumpkin. I started making this a few years ago in the fall—the bite that the ginger adds to the hummus makes it taste very autumnal. It is a really pretty addition to any table, with its orange hue set off by hot pink pomegranate seeds and bright green cilantro leaves. Confession: I have made a version of this by just stirring pumpkin puree into store-bought hummus, so try that if you're in a rush.

Two 15-ounce (425 g) cans chickpeas, drained and liquid reserved

One 15-ounce (425 g) can pure pumpkin puree

¼ cup (60 ml) tahini

1-inch (2.5 cm) piece fresh ginger, minced

1 clove garlic, minced

Juice of 1 lemon

1 teaspoon ground cumin

¼ cup (60 ml) extra-virgin olive oil, plus more for drizzling

1 teaspoon kosher salt

¼ teaspoon freshly ground black pepper

2 tablespoons fresh pomegranate seeds

Fresh cilantro leaves

Pita chips and crudités, for serving

In a food processor, combine the chickpeas, pumpkin, tahini, ginger, garlic, lemon juice, and cumin. Process until smooth. With the motor running, slowly pour in the oil in a steady stream. Add the salt and pepper and process until very smooth. If the mixture is too thick, add some of the chickpea liquid, about 2 tablespoons at a time, until the desired consistency is reached.

Transfer to a serving dish and drizzle with oil. Garnish with the pomegranate seeds and cilantro leaves. Serve with pita chips and crudités.

Fig and Pepita Goat Cheese Log

This is one of those dishes that is so simple, yet you just can't stop eating it. Sweet and salty always wins! You can substitute different kinds of jams and nuts as well. I like this with apricot jam and chopped pistachios, or a drizzle of honey and a sprinkle of cracked black pepper and chopped almonds. I especially enjoy this nibble with a glass of bubbly.

YIELD
8 to 10 servings

ACTIVE TIME
5 minutes

TOTAL TIME
5 minutes

One 10½-ounce (300 g) log goat cheese

¼ cup (60 ml) fig jam

½ cup (30 g) roasted salted pepitas (hulled pumpkin seeds)

Kosher salt and freshly ground black pepper

Crackers, for serving

Place the goat cheese log on a cheese board, plate, or platter. Spoon the fig jam over the goat cheese, gently spreading it with the back of the spoon. Sprinkle the pepitas over the fig jam to coat. Season with salt and pepper to taste and serve with crackers.

Celery with Cream Cheese and Everything Bagel Seasoning

YIELD
4 servings

TOTAL TIME
5 minutes

I truly think I would eat cardboard if it had everything bagel seasoning on it. How did we make it so many years without someone thinking of bottling and selling the stuff until recently? Now, it's everywhere! I love it on my popcorn, I put it on salmon, sometimes I even put it on the cream cheese on an everything bagel. I'm extra like that. This recipe might be one of the quickest hors d'oeuvres I have in this collection and also one of the most satisfying.

3 ribs celery, cut into four equal pieces each

3 ounces (85 g) cream cheese

Everything bagel seasoning

Spread cream cheese onto each piece of celery. Sprinkle with everything bagel seasoning and serve.

Blue Cheese–Stuffed Dates

Salty-sweet cannot be beat! Funky, creamy blue cheese stuffed inside a sweet date is such a great combo. You can wrap it in bacon or prosciutto and bake it if you want to go one more step, or if blue cheese isn't your thing, try it with goat cheese or Manchego.

15 to 20 pitted dates

½ cup (70 g) crumbled good-quality
    blue cheese

Cut a slit into one side of each date, exposing the cavity. Fill the cavity of the date with cheese. Serve at room temperature or refrigerate until ready to serve.

YIELD
4 to 6 servings

TOTAL TIME
10 minutes

Prosciutto Crisps

Salty, porky, crispy prosciutto. What's not to love about that? Very often for cocktail hour, I do a prosciutto and Parmesan plate with Aperol Spritzes. To add a little twist, I'll serve some prosciutto as is, and some crisped in the oven. Make extra crisps and have them with eggs in the morning, or crumbled on a salad or on a simple plate of buttered pasta tossed with Parmesan.

2 ounces (55 g) thinly sliced prosciutto

Preheat the oven to 400°F (205°C). Line a baking sheet with parchment paper.

Arrange the prosciutto on the prepared baking sheet so that the slices are not touching. Bake for 6 to 8 minutes, until very crisp. Let cool completely on the baking sheet. Serve immediately or store in an airtight container.

YIELD
4 servings

TOTAL TIME
10 minutes

Crispy Artichoke Hearts

YIELD

About 20 pieces

ACTIVE TIME

10 minutes

TOTAL TIME

40 minutes

Fried nibbles with cocktails are always a treat, but it can be messy to fry at home and can feel like a waste of oil for something small like these artichoke hearts. I like to create my own "air fryer" in my oven by using a rack on a baking sheet and setting my oven to convection. If you don't have a convection setting, regular works just fine. You can try this same cracker crumb mixture on chicken tenders.

14 round salted butter crackers

4 fresh basil leaves

2 tablespoons finely grated Parmesan cheese

1 tablespoon fresh flat-leaf parsley leaves

¼ teaspoon garlic salt

One 24-ounce (680 g) jar marinated quartered artichoke hearts, drained

Marinara sauce, for serving (optional)

Toothpicks

Preheat the oven to 425°F (220°C) on convection setting, if available. Place a wire cooling rack on a baking sheet and spray with nonstick cooking spray.

In a food processor, combine the crackers, basil, cheese, parsley, and garlic salt and process to fine crumbs (the texture of breadcrumbs). Roll the artichoke hearts in the cracker crumb mixture and place on the prepared rack.

Bake until the cracker crumbs are golden brown, about 30 minutes. Arrange the artichokes on a serving platter with toothpicks. Serve with marinara sauce for dipping, if desired.

Iced Peach Bourbon
Lemonade Tea, page 13

Herbed Cheese with
Crostini and Radishes, page 32

Pumpkin Hummus,
page 24

Cosmo Americano,
page 16

Celery with Cream Cheese and
Everything Bagel Seasoning,
page 26

Herbed Cheese with Crostini and Radishes

YIELD
4 to 6 servings

TOTAL TIME
20 minutes

Radishes are so lovely during cocktail hour, not only because they're tasty and usually served in a salty manner, making them a good partner to a stiff drink, but also because they're so bright, pretty, and festive. Often I serve them simply with butter and salt, but I like to go the extra mile by making this simple herbed cheese spread for crostini and topping each one with a thin slice of radish.

½ baguette, cut on a bias into ¼-inch (6 mm) slices

2 tablespoons extra-virgin olive oil

4 ounces (115 g) goat cheese, at room temperature

4 ounces (115 g) cream cheese, at room temperature

¼ teaspoon garlic powder

¼ teaspoon kosher salt

¼ teaspoon cracked black pepper

2 tablespoons fresh parsley leaves, chopped

2 tablespoons fresh mint leaves, chopped

2 tablespoons chopped fresh chives

3 to 4 watermelon radishes, or breakfast or globe radishes, very thinly sliced

Preheat the oven to 400°F (205°C).

Place the baguette slices on a rimmed baking sheet. Brush or drizzle with oil. Bake for 10 to 15 minutes, until golden brown.

Mix the cheeses, garlic powder, salt, and pepper with an electric mixer in a large bowl until very creamy and combined. Stir in the parsley, mint, and chives until just combined. Spread the cheese mixture onto the crostini, top with the radishes, and serve.

Hot Roasted Eggplant Dip

So here's the deal: Cream cheese and mayonnaise are a match made in heaven when it comes to making a dip. You can add just about anything, like jarred roasted red peppers, spinach and artichokes, or mushrooms for your flavoring. Then add cheese and bake it. Voilà: You have a spectacular dip that everyone will be swarming around. For this rendition, I added roasted eggplant, and it's out of this world with some pita chips or spread on toasted baguette.

YIELD
4 to 6 servings

ACTIVE TIME
5 minutes

TOTAL TIME
30 minutes

½ eggplant, skin on, cubed (about 3 cups/240 g)

2 tablespoons olive oil

Kosher salt and freshly ground black pepper

2 cloves garlic

One 8-ounce (226 g) package cream cheese, at room temperature

½ cup (120 ml) mayonnaise

½ cup (50 g) grated Parmesan cheese

½ teaspoon kosher salt

¼ teaspoon freshly ground black pepper

6 large fresh basil leaves

¼ cup (30 g) shredded mozzarella cheese

Toasted baguette slices or pita chips

Preheat the oven to 450°F (230°C). Line a baking sheet with parchment paper.

Put the eggplant in a large bowl and slowly drizzle with 1 tablespoon of the oil. Stir and drizzle in an additional tablespoon of oil. Season generously with salt and pepper and toss to combine. Spread out on the prepared baking sheet. Bake for 10 minutes, then stir and bake for an additional 10 minutes.

Reduce the oven temperature to 350°F (175°C). Grease a 2-quart (2 L) baking dish with cooking spray.

In a food processor, blend the roasted eggplant and the garlic until combined. Add the cream cheese, mayo, Parmesan, salt, pepper, and basil to the processor and blend. Spoon into the prepared baking dish. Top with the mozzarella. Bake until bubbling and the top is golden brown, 20 to 25 minutes. Serve with toasted baguette slices or pita chips.

Bloody Mary Shrimp Cocktail "Ceviche" with Plantain Chips

YIELD
4 servings

ACTIVE TIME
15 minutes

TOTAL TIME
4 hours 15 minutes
(includes marinating time)

Ceviche is one of those things that can be a little intimidating to make at home. Not because it's difficult (quite the opposite, actually), but because it can leave you with a lot of questions, namely "When is it *done*?" And if you live in an area where it's a challenge to find really fresh seafood, you might be hesitant to want to eat it essentially raw. Enter this shrimp cocktail ceviche, which uses cooked shrimp. You still get that great citrusy fresh flavor but without any guesswork. Serve this on a summer day with an ice-cold beer or an orange shandy, or in the winter when you want to feel like you're on vacation.

1 pound (455 g) frozen peeled cooked shrimp (16- to 20-count), thawed, tails removed, cut into ¼-inch (6 mm) pieces

¾ cup (180 ml) Bloody Mary mix

1½ teaspoons celery salt

Juice of 1 lime

2 tablespoons minced fresh cilantro

2 tablespoons minced red onion

1 avocado, diced

Hot sauce (optional)

Kosher salt and freshly ground black pepper

Plantain chips, for serving

In a large nonreactive mixing bowl, combine the shrimp with the Bloody Mary mix, 1 teaspoon of the celery salt, and half of the lime juice. Cover and refrigerate for 3 to 4 hours.

Drain the shrimp and reserve 2 tablespoons of the liquid. Transfer the shrimp and the reserved liquid to a medium bowl. Add the cilantro, onion, avocado, the remaining ½ teaspoon celery salt, the remaining lime juice, a few dashes of hot sauce if desired, and salt and pepper to taste. Serve with plantain chips.

*Bloody Mary Shrimp Cocktail "Ceviche"
with Plantain Chips, page 35*

Iceberg Disk Salad

40

Grilled Sweet Potato and Arugula Salad

42

Arugula, Fennel, and Citrus Salad

43

Shaved Brussels Sprouts Salad

45

Greek Salad with Creamy Feta Dressing

46

Roasted Carrots and Red Leaf Lettuce Salad with Ranch Dressing

49

Roasted Beet and Beet Green Salad with Herbs, Goat Cheese, and Bacon

50

Spicy Kale Caesar with Crispy Onions, Almonds, Avocado, and Croutons

53

Pesto Farro with Smoked Mozzarella, Arugula, Corn, and Tomatoes

54

Purple Cauliflower and Red Cabbage Salad

57

Lobster Cobb

58

Grilled Tuna Salad with Miso-Carrot-Ginger Dressing

61

Oil and Vinegar Herbed Potato Salad

62

Red Curry Lentil and Squash Stew

65

Chipotle Carrot Soup

66

Broccoli Green Curry Coconut Soup

67

Creamy Parmesan Cauliflower Soup

68

Cannellini and Escarole Soup

71

Harissa Butternut Squash Soup

72

White Chicken Chili

73

Classic Chicken Noodle Soup

74

chapter two

———

SALADS AND SOUPS

Iceberg Disk Salad

YIELD
4 servings

TOTAL TIME
10 minutes

Steakhouse dining will always be high on my list, not so much because I love steak, but because I love iceberg wedge salad and all the sides. I find that a wedge salad is a little cumbersome to get into, and since there's not as much surface space on the lettuce, some bites have less of the star ingredient than others. I'm talking about the blue cheese dressing, of course. If you slice the head of lettuce into disks, the dressing can get down into all the crevices for maximum blue cheese enjoyment.

1 head iceberg lettuce, cut into four round slices through the "equator"

Blue Cheese Dressing (recipe follows)

1 cup (145 g) cherry tomatoes, cut into quarters

6 slices cooked bacon, crumbled or chopped

¼ cup (11 g) thinly sliced fresh chives

Divide the lettuce rounds among four plates. Pour ¼ cup (60 ml) of the dressing over each. Top with the tomatoes and bacon and sprinkle with the chives. Serve immediately.

Blue Cheese Dressing
YIELD: 1½ CUPS (355 ML)

Oh, blue cheese dressing, how I love thee. I did my best to mimic my favorite steakhouse dressing here and I really do think the key is to buy a hunk of blue cheese and crumble it yourself, not a tub of the already crumbled stuff. It's richer and creamier and all around more flavor-packed.

6 ounces (170 g) blue cheese, crumbled, at room temperature

⅓ cup (75 ml) vegetable oil

⅔ cup (165 ml) mayonnaise

2 tablespoons white wine vinegar

1 tablespoon hot sauce, such as Crystal or Louisiana, plus more if desired

Kosher salt and cracked black pepper

In a medium bowl, whisk together the blue cheese, oil, mayonnaise, vinegar, and hot sauce. Season with salt and pepper and add more hot sauce if preferred. Set aside.

Grilled Sweet Potato and Arugula Salad

YIELD
6 to 8 servings

ACTIVE TIME
20 minutes

TOTAL TIME
25 minutes

This was a dish born of necessity when I was preparing for a last-minute barbecue and needed a side dish. Now it is in my permanent rotation. The recipe is pretty versatile. You can also roast the sweet potatoes in the oven and add a garnish of pomegranates. I have even made it more like a regular-potato salad by increasing the sweet potatoes, dicing and roasting them, and decreasing the arugula.

- 2 large sweet potatoes, skin-on, sliced ¼ inch (6 mm) thick
- 1 tablespoon extra-virgin olive oil
- Kosher salt and freshly ground black pepper
- 6 cups (120 g) loosely packed baby arugula
- 4 scallions, white and light green parts only, thinly sliced
- ¼ cup (60 ml) mayonnaise
- 2 tablespoons fresh lemon juice
- 2 tablespoons grated Parmesan cheese

Preheat a grill or grill pan to medium.

Toss the sweet potatoes in a large bowl with the oil, ½ teaspoon salt, and ¼ teaspoon pepper. Transfer to the grill or grill pan and cook for 3 to 4 minutes per side, until fork tender. (You may need to flip and cook an additional couple of minutes, depending on your grill heat.) Let cool to room temperature.

In a large bowl, combine the arugula, cooked sweet potatoes, and scallions. In a small bowl, whisk the mayonnaise with the lemon juice and Parmesan; season with salt and pepper. Just before serving, toss the dressing with the sweet potato and arugula mixture to coat.

Arugula, Fennel, and Citrus Salad

YIELD
4 servings

TOTAL TIME
15 minutes

This is one of my favorite winter salads. The fennel and orange make it a perfect accompaniment to a fish dinner (great with just a piece of grilled or baked salmon), and the bright pop of color from the pomegranate makes it feel festive on a holiday buffet.

4 cups (80 g) loosely packed arugula

3 tablespoons chopped toasted walnuts

1 fennel bulb, thinly sliced, plus 1 tablespoon chopped fronds for garnish

1 orange, segmented, plus the juice squeezed from the hull

Seeds from 1 pomegranate

½ red onion, thinly sliced

1 tablespoon Dijon mustard

1 tablespoon balsamic vinegar

3 tablespoons extra-virgin olive oil

Kosher salt and freshly ground black pepper

Toss the arugula, walnuts, sliced fennel, orange segments, pomegranate seeds, and onion together in a large bowl.

Whisk together the mustard, vinegar, and orange juice in a small bowl. Whisk in the oil. Season with salt and pepper.

Drizzle the salad with the dressing to taste. Garnish with fennel fronds and serve immediately.

Shaved Brussels Sprouts Salad

If I were to make a list of my top-ten successful recipes, this salad would be on it. The dressing is bright and lemony; the sprouts are crunchy, with their bitterness perfectly balanced out by the sweet dates and creamy Manchego. I came up with the idea for it a few years ago around Thanksgiving. I find that everything else in the traditional meal is so heavy on the plate, and this salad adds the perfect pop of flavor. Bonus: You don't have to take up any of that valuable oven space. If you want to stretch the salad, add a bag of arugula.

YIELD
6 to 8 servings

ACTIVE TIME
10 minutes

TOTAL TIME
15 minutes

½ cup (120 ml) fresh lemon juice

2 tablespoons minced shallots

1 tablespoon Dijon mustard

1 tablespoon honey

½ cup (120 ml) extra-virgin olive oil

Kosher salt and freshly cracked black pepper

1 pound (455 g) Brussels sprouts, stems trimmed

¼ cup (35 g) chopped dates

¼ cup (35 g) diced Manchego cheese

¼ cup (35 g) chopped almonds

In a small bowl, combine the lemon juice and shallots. Let stand for 5 minutes, so the acidity in the lemon juice can begin to break down the shallots. Whisk in the mustard and honey until well combined. Slowly whisk in the oil until emulsified. Season aggressively with salt and add pepper to taste.

In a food processor fitted with the slicing blade, process the sprouts until all are thinly sliced. (Alternatively, use a knife to thinly slice them, or buy a bag of already sliced sprouts in the produce section of your grocery store.)

Add the sprouts, dates, cheese, and almonds to a salad bowl, drizzle with the dressing, and toss to coat. The salad can be dressed 15 to 20 minutes in advance if you like more tender Brussels sprouts.

Greek Salad with Creamy Feta Dressing

YIELD
4 servings

TOTAL TIME
10 minutes

About six or seven years ago, my friend Suzanne and I made a Greek salad together. We still talk about that salad. Neither one of us can figure out what made it so perfect. We used a really good feta cheese and olives, but perhaps it was the summer tomatoes, or the freshly picked lettuce we got from the farm stand. Whatever it was, it was magic. Recently I tried mixing up my Greek salad game by making a creamy feta dressing instead of just adding feta crumbles. Whoa, Nelly! Success! With a feta dressing, you get feta flavor in every bite, and you don't have to just pick through the salad trying to find the cheese (this is me). Suzanne, this recipe gives our Greek salad of yesteryear a run for its money.

¼ cup (60 ml) extra-virgin olive oil

¼ cup (60 ml) red wine vinegar

1 cup (150 g) crumbled feta cheese

½ teaspoon dried oregano

½ teaspoon sugar

Pinch of kosher salt

2 to 3 romaine lettuce hearts, chopped

¼ cup (40 g) pitted Kalamata olives, sliced

1 cup (135 g) grape tomatoes, halved

½ red onion, sliced

¼ cup (35 g) sliced pepperoncini

Put the oil, vinegar, feta, oregano, sugar, and salt in a blender. Blend until very smooth. Put the lettuce in a large bowl, pour the dressing over, and toss until coated. Transfer to a serving bowl and top with the olives, tomatoes, onion, and pepperoncini. Serve immediately.

Roasted Carrots and Red Leaf Lettuce Salad with Ranch Dressing

YIELD
4 to 6 servings

ACTIVE TIME
15 minutes

TOTAL TIME
45 minutes
(includes cooling time)

Adding a roasted vegetable into a leafy green salad is a great way to bring some dimension to what could otherwise be a boring salad. Greens with raw carrots? Blah. Greens with roasted carrots, cheddar cheese, sunflower seeds, and cherries? Helloooo! Oh, and did I mention there's ranch? I'd eat just about anything with ranch dressing. I like to use carrots that have their tops because they add so much flavor to the salad. They're one of those things that we tend to just automatically throw away, but give them a try and you'll find that they're really good. I also use them in vinaigrettes and to make carrot top pesto. Treat them just as you would an herb.

1 small bunch carrots with leafy green tops

2 tablespoons olive oil

1 tablespoon honey

½ teaspoon sea salt

¼ teaspoon freshly ground black pepper

1 head red leaf lettuce, torn into pieces

3 tablespoons roasted salted sunflower seeds

3 tablespoons chopped dried cherries

3 ounces (85 g) crumbled extra-sharp cheddar cheese

Ranch Dressing (recipe follows)

Preheat the oven to 450°F (230°C). Line a baking sheet with parchment paper.

Cut the green leaves from the carrot tops, then rinse, drain, and set them aside. Use a vegetable brush to clean the carrots (leave the peel on to give the carrots texture). Cut them on the diagonal into 1-inch (2.5 cm) pieces.

In a small bowl, toss the carrots with the oil, honey, salt, and pepper. Transfer to the prepared baking sheet and roast until tender and caramelized (I like mine to be on the borderline of burned), about 20 minutes. Let cool completely.

Chop the reserved carrot leaves to make 2 tablespoons. In a large salad bowl, toss the lettuce, carrot leaves, sunflower seeds, cherries, cheese, and carrots with desired amount of ranch dressing. Serve immediately.

Ranch Dressing
YIELD: ABOUT 1¼ CUPS (300 ML)

1 cup (240 ml) mayonnaise

½ cup (120 ml) buttermilk

2 tablespoons minced fresh chives

2 tablespoons minced fresh flat-leaf parsley

¼ teaspoon salt

¼ teaspoon freshly ground black pepper

¼ teaspoon garlic powder

In a bowl, combine all the ingredients and mix well. Refrigerate, for up to 1 week, until serving.

Roasted Beet and Beet Green Salad with Herbs, Goat Cheese, and Bacon

YIELD
4 servings

ACTIVE TIME
20 minutes

TOTAL TIME
1 hour

Beet greens are another one of those things that we tend to throw out, but they're so good! You can eat them raw in a salad, like this one, or sauté them with some onions and garlic for a quick side dish. If you want to make this dish extra rich, save a tablespoon of fat from the bacon when you cook it and whisk it into your dressing.

3 beets, peeled and cut into 1-inch wedges, plus beet greens, roughly chopped

1 tablespoon olive oil

Kosher salt and cracked black pepper

3 cups (60 g) baby kale

¼ cup (13 g) fresh parsley leaves

¼ cup (10 g) fresh cilantro leaves

¼ cup (13 g) fresh mint leaves

4 ounces (115 g) goat cheese, crumbled

4 slices cooked bacon, crumbled or chopped

¼ cup (45 g) pomegranate seeds

¼ cup (30 g) roasted pistachios, roughly chopped

House Dressing (recipe follows)

Preheat the oven to 400°F (205°C). Line a baking sheet with parchment paper.

In a bowl, toss the beets with the oil and season with salt and pepper. Transfer to the prepared baking sheet. Bake until the beets are tender, 30 to 40 minutes.

In a large salad bowl, toss the beet greens with the baby kale and herbs. Top with the warm roasted beets, the goat cheese, bacon, pomegranate seeds, pistachios, and dressing to taste. Serve immediately.

House Dressing (Dijon Vinaigrette)

YIELD: ABOUT 1½ CUPS (360 ML)

This is my go-to salad dressing. The ratio to remember is 1 part acid to 3 parts oil. You can use white wine vinegar, lemon juice, apple cider vinegar—any acid you like to any oil you prefer—olive oil, avocado oil, you name it. I like a little honey to balance it out, but a pinch of sugar or maple syrup works as well. If you want to make a single serving for one big salad, just do 1 tablespoon vinegar to 3 tablespoons oil, with Dijon and honey to taste.

⅓ cup (75 ml) red wine vinegar

2 tablespoons Dijon mustard

1 teaspoon honey

1 cup (240 ml) extra-virgin olive oil

Kosher salt and freshly ground black pepper

In a small bowl, whisk vinegar, mustard, and honey until emulsified. Slowly drizzle in the olive oil as you continue to whisk. Whisk until completely emulsified. Season generously with salt and pepper and whisk. Store in an airtight container until serving.

Spicy Kale Caesar with Crispy Onions, Almonds, Avocado, and Croutons

YIELD
4 to 6 servings

TOTAL TIME
30 minutes

Everyone who knows me knows I *love* kale. Some of the crew members on *The Kitchen* even got me a T-shirt emblazoned with "KALE" in the same style as "YALE." I am currently living for the spicy kale salad at my neighborhood restaurant the Butcher's Daughter. I've done my best to re-create it here. I think the secret is the fried onions; I'm sure the restaurant makes them in-house, but store-bought ones work well here too.

For the salad:

2 bunches curly kale, stemmed and roughly chopped

Juice of 1 lemon

1 avocado, sliced

¼ cup (14 g) French fried onions

¼ cup (25 g) sliced almonds, toasted

¼ cup (25 g) grated Parmesan cheese

For the croutons:

2 tablespoons unsalted butter, melted

2 tablespoons extra-virgin olive oil

½ teaspoon paprika

½ teaspoon garlic salt

2 cups (53 g) torn baguette pieces

For the dressing:

Juice of 1 lemon

½ cup (120 ml) mayonnaise

2 teaspoons sambal

1 tablespoon honey

2 dashes Worcestershire sauce

Pinch of kosher salt

Pinch of cracked black pepper

Preheat the oven to 400°F (205°C). Line a baking sheet with parchment paper.

Start the salad: Put the kale in a large bowl. Add the lemon juice and gently massage it into the leaves. Set aside while making the croutons and the dressing, 10 to 20 minutes.

Make the croutons: Stir the butter, oil, paprika, and garlic salt together in a medium bowl. Toss the baguette in the mixture until all the pieces are coated. Spread the baguette onto the prepared baking sheet. Bake for 5 to 7 minutes, until the croutons are crispy and golden brown.

Make the dressing: Whisk all the ingredients in a small bowl until well combined.

Toss the kale with the dressing and top with the avocado, croutons, fried onions, almonds, and cheese. Serve immediately.

Pesto Farro with Smoked Mozzarella, Arugula, Corn, and Tomatoes

---

YIELD
4 servings

ACTIVE TIME
10 minutes

TOTAL TIME
45 minutes

This is the ultimate summer buffet salad. It's so easy to make ahead of time—just toss all of the ingredients except the arugula together in advance, then add the arugula just before serving so it stays nice and fresh. The corn, cut straight from the cob, adds a burst of sweetness in each bite. If you want to make this a main dish, add grilled chicken or shrimp, or even roasted chickpeas for a vegetarian option.

1 cup (200 g) farro

One 7-ounce (200 g) container pesto

Zest and juice of 1 lemon

1 pint (270 g) grape tomatoes, halved

2 ears corn, kernels cut from the cob

2 Persian cucumbers, diced

2 scallions, white and light green parts, thinly sliced

7 ounces (200 g) smoked mozzarella, cubed

Kosher salt and freshly ground black pepper

4 cups (80 G) loosely packed baby arugula

Grated Parmesan cheese

Cook the farro according to the package instructions. Let cool completely. (I like to spread the farro out on a sheet pan so it cools faster.)

In a large bowl, whisk the pesto together with the lemon zest and juice. Toss with the farro, then add the tomatoes, corn, cucumbers, scallions, and mozzarella. Season with salt and pepper. Toss in the arugula, sprinkle with Parmesan, and serve.

Purple Cauliflower and Red Cabbage Salad

YIELD
4 to 6 servings

TOTAL TIME
10 minutes

This salad adds an unusually colorful pop to a buffet spread. It is so crunchy and fresh, and I love the combo of the bitter cauliflower and cabbage and the sweet poppyseed dressing. Roasted and salted sunflower seeds are a welcome addition to any salad, in my opinion, especially this one. In the fall and early winter when these vegetables are in season, it's not necessarily the norm to serve them raw, so it's a really nice change of pace.

3 cups (about ½ head/285 g) thinly sliced purple cauliflower

3 cups (about ½ head/285 g) shredded red cabbage

½ recipe Poppyseed Dressing (page 57)

5 tablespoons (45 g) roasted salted sunflower seeds

Toss the cauliflower and cabbage with the dressing until fully coated. Sprinkle with sunflower seeds. Serve immediately or refrigerate up to overnight.

Poppyseed Dressing
YIELD: ABOUT 1¼ CUPS (300 ML)

⅔ cup (165 ml) canola oil

⅓ cup (75 ml) apple cider vinegar

3 tablespoons honey

2 tablespoons Dijon mustard

1 large egg

Kosher salt and cracked black pepper

2 tablespoons poppyseeds

Put the oil, vinegar, honey, mustard, egg, ½ teaspoon salt, and ¼ teaspoon pepper in a blender and blend until smooth. Use a spatula to stir in the poppyseeds, then season with more salt and pepper if needed. Refrigerate until ready to serve.

Lobster Cobb

YIELD
4 to 6
servings

TOTAL TIME
10 minutes

Out at the end of Long Island is a small town called Montauk. When I first moved to the area, it was a fairly quiet commercial fishing community. Fast-forward to today, it's become the hip, trendy place to be. For years, I would go to the waterside restaurant Duryea's to order a lobster at the counter, sit at a picnic table, and watch the sunset. It was as low-frills as they come, but everything you wanted it to be. As it so happens, Duryea's was sold. I heard it was reopening under new management and feared that it would be just another spot for the cool kids. While it is certainly much more polished these days, the food is excellent. They make a giant lobster Cobb salad that inspired me to make my own version. You can also make this recipe with shrimp or crab.

¼ cup (60 ml) mayonnaise

1 tablespoon fresh tarragon, chopped

2 tablespoons fresh lemon juice

8 ounces (225 g) cooked lobster meat (or cooked shrimp, crab, or even chicken)

Kosher salt and cracked black pepper

½ shallot, minced

2 tablespoons Dijon mustard

2 tablespoons white wine vinegar

6 tablespoons (90 ml) extra-virgin olive oil

2 heads romaine lettuce hearts, chopped

1 cup (135 g) grape tomatoes, halved

Two 6-minute boiled eggs (page 197), peeled and quartered

1 avocado, diced

4 slices cooked bacon, diced

½ cup (70 g) crumbled good-quality blue cheese

Gently stir together the mayonnaise, tarragon, and lemon juice. Fold in the lobster. Season with a pinch of salt and pepper.

Whisk together the shallot, mustard, and vinegar in a large salad bowl. Slowly stream in the oil while whisking. Toss the lettuce with the dressing, then arrange the lobster mixture, tomatoes, eggs, avocado, bacon, and cheese on top of the lettuce in neat rows. Serve immediately.

Grilled Tuna Salad with Miso-Carrot-Ginger Dressing

YIELD
4 to 6 servings

TOTAL TIME
20 minutes

This is my version of a sushi restaurant sashimi salad. I always love the salad dressing at sushi restaurants, so I did my best to make my own version. It's really easy and really tasty, plus you get a serving of carrots, so bonus vitamins in there! I like at least a little sear on my tuna instead of straight sashimi style. This recipe is also delicious with grilled salmon. The crunch of the wonton crisps is my favorite part.

For the tuna:

1 pound (455 g) very fresh tuna steaks (2 to 3 steaks; about 1 inch/ 2.5 cm thick)

1 tablespoon extra-virgin olive oil

Kosher salt and freshly ground black pepper

For the dressing:

2 medium carrots, chopped

1-inch (2.5 c) piece fresh ginger, chopped

¼ cup (60 ml) rice vinegar

2 tablespoons white miso paste

2 tablespoons vegetable oil or avocado oil

2 teaspoons honey

2 teaspoons toasted sesame oil

For the salad:

8 cups (320 g) mesclun salad greens

1 English cucumber, cut in half lengthwise and thinly sliced

1 red bell pepper, thinly sliced

1 cup (110 g) wonton crisps

Make the tuna: Preheat an outdoor grill or a grill pan to medium-high. Drizzle the tuna with the oil and generously season with salt and pepper on both sides. Grill for about 2 minutes on each side. Remove from the grill, tent with foil, and let stand for a few minutes. Thinly slice.

Make the dressing: Put the carrots, ginger, vinegar, miso paste, vegetable oil, honey, sesame oil, and 2 tablespoons water in a blender and blend until smooth.

Make the salad: In a large salad bowl, combine the salad greens, cucumber, and bell pepper. Add ¼ cup (60 ml) of the dressing and toss to coat. Top with the sliced tuna and wonton crisps and serve with additional dressing on the side.

Oil and Vinegar Herbed Potato Salad

YIELD

4 to 6 servings

TOTAL TIME

45 minutes

Salt and vinegar chips are my kryptonite, and this potato salad is like their grown-up, sophisticated cousin. I toss the new potatoes in the vinaigrette while they are still hot, then let them cool to room temperature before adding in the fresh herbs so they stay bright green. In the summer, this is great for a buffet, unlike the salad's mayonnaise-dressed counterpart, which can spoil quickly in the heat. Alternatively, because it's warm, it's perfect for the winter. Serve it with a roast pork and sauerkraut, or as a side with my Pork Chops with White Beans, Fennel, and Onions (page 95).

3 pounds (1.4 kg) red new potatoes, cut into 1- to 1½-inch (2.5 to 4 cm) pieces

Kosher salt

½ cup (120 ml) extra-virgin olive oil

¼ cup (60 ml) white wine vinegar

2 tablespoons stone-ground mustard

½ teaspoon cracked black pepper

1 shallot, minced

2 tablespoons chopped fresh chives

2 tablespoons chopped fresh dill

2 tablespoons chopped fresh parsley

In a large saucepan, cover the potatoes with 1 inch (2.5 cm) of cold water. Add 2 tablespoons kosher salt. Bring to a simmer and cook for 35 minutes, until the potatoes are very tender. Drain well.

In a large bowl, mix the oil, vinegar, mustard, 2 teaspoons salt, the pepper, and shallot. Toss the hot potatoes in the dressing. Let cool slightly, 5 to 10 minutes, then sprinkle with the herbs and toss to coat. Serve warm or at room temperature, or refrigerate until ready to serve.

Red Curry Lentil and Squash Stew

This is one of my all-time favorite comfort foods, a true "laze around on a cold night and watch TV" dish. It is so hearty and satisfying, and the kitchen smells amazing as it fills with the aroma of curry, garlic, and ginger. Ryan laughs at me because I will eat all of the leftovers of this stew myself. I could eat it every day for five days and be perfectly happy.

YIELD
6 to 8 servings

ACTIVE TIME
20 minutes

TOTAL TIME
1 hour and 35 minutes

1 tablespoon coconut oil

1 yellow onion, diced

1 carrot, diced

1 rib celery, diced

3 cloves garlic, minced

1 tablespoon minced fresh ginger

1 tablespoon curry powder

2 cups (230 g) cubed butternut squash

2 teaspoons kosher salt

½ teaspoon freshly ground black pepper

1 cup (200 g) red lentils

One 14½-ounce (411 g) can diced tomatoes

1 bay leaf

4 cups (960 ml) vegetable stock

One 13½-ounce (400 ml) can coconut milk

2 cups (40 g) loosely packed baby spinach

For garnish: plain yogurt, cilantro, hot sauce, lime

Heat the coconut oil in a Dutch oven over medium-high heat. Add the onion, carrot, and celery. Cook until tender, 8 to 10 minutes, stirring occasionally. Stir in the garlic, ginger, and curry powder. Cook for 1 to 2 minutes, taking care not to let the garlic burn. Stir in the squash, salt, and pepper. Add the lentils, tomatoes, bay leaf, stock, and coconut milk. Bring to a simmer, then reduce the heat to low. Cover and cook for 1 hour. Stir in the spinach and cook for 10 to 15 minutes. Serve garnished with yogurt, cilantro, hot sauce, and lime.

Chipotle Carrot Soup

YIELD
4 to 6 servings

TOTAL TIME
30 minutes

This carrot soup is like the red-orange version of my Broccoli Green Curry Coconut Soup (page 67). I always have a jar of both red curry paste and green curry paste in my fridge, and the pantry is always stocked with canned coconut milk. So depending what vegetables are in the crisper, that's the soup that's getting made. The spices and the rich coconut milk make a soup that's relatively quick to make taste like it took hours.

1 tablespoon olive oil

1 yellow onion, diced

2 cloves garlic, minced

½ teaspoon ground cumin

1 tablespoon adobo chile sauce (from a can of chipotle chiles)

2 bunches carrots, scrubbed, tops removed, cut into chunks

2 teaspoons kosher salt

4 cups (960 ml) vegetable stock or chicken stock

Juice of 1 lime

For garnish: fresh cilantro leaves, crumbled queso fresco, and toasted pumpkin seeds

Heat the oil in a Dutch oven or large, heavy-bottomed saucepan over medium-high heat. Add the onion and cook, stirring frequently, until the onion starts to soften, 3 to 4 minutes. Add the garlic, cumin, and adobo and cook for 1 minute, or until very fragrant. Add the carrots and salt and stir until everything is fully coated in curry. Pour in the stock. Bring to a simmer and cook for 15 minutes, or until the carrots are tender. Remove from the heat and add the lime juice. Transfer the soup to a blender or use an immersion blender to blend until smooth. Top each serving with cilantro, cheese, and pumpkin seeds.

Broccoli Green Curry Coconut Soup

YIELD
4 to 6 servings

TOTAL TIME
30 minutes

I think of pureed soups like smoothies—I'm packing a lot of nutrients into one meal, blending it up, and having a tasty treat that is also good for me. I use the same base with many different versions of soup. I always sauté an onion and garlic, then add the veggie of choice, some flavoring, and the stock, then blend. This broccoli soup is pretty heavenly with the combination of green curry and coconut milk.

1 tablespoon coconut oil

1 yellow onion, diced

2 tablespoons minced fresh ginger

2 cloves garlic, minced

2 tablespoons green curry paste

2 bunches broccoli, stalks and florets, chopped

2 teaspoons kosher salt

2 cups (480 ml) vegetable stock

One 13½-ounce (400 ml) can coconut milk

¼ cup (10 g) loosely packed cilantro leaves, plus more for serving

Juice of 1 lime

For garnish: fresh Thai basil, chopped peanuts, sliced Fresno chiles

Melt the coconut oil in a Dutch oven or large, heavy-bottomed saucepan over medium-high heat. Add the onion and cook, stirring frequently, until the onion starts to soften, 3 to 4 minutes. Add the ginger, garlic, and curry paste and cook for 1 minute, or until very fragrant. Add the broccoli and salt and stir until everything is fully coated in curry. Pour in the stock and coconut milk. Bring to a simmer and cook for 15 minutes, or until the broccoli is tender. Remove from the heat and add the cilantro and lime juice. Transfer the soup to a blender or use an immersion blender to blend until smooth. Top with Thai basil, peanuts, cilantro, and chiles, or your favorite toppings!

Creamy Parmesan Cauliflower Soup

YIELD
4 to 6 servings

TOTAL TIME
30 minutes

This cauliflower soup is so velvety and creamy no one would ever guess that it's free from heavy cream. The Parmesan rind infuses the stock with salty umami flavor, and the addition of the cheese at the end enriches the flavor even more. I am addicted to those Parmesan crisps they sell in the cheese section (it's hard for me to even buy a package because I eat them so quickly!), and they make a great topping for this soup. Or you can top with Prosciutto Crisps (page 14).

1 tablespoon olive oil

1 yellow onion, diced

2 tablespoons minced fresh ginger

2 cloves garlic, minced

2 heads cauliflower, cored and chopped

2 teaspoons kosher salt

4 cups (960 ml) vegetable stock or chicken stock

1-inch (2.5 cm) piece Parmesan rind

⅓ cup (30 g) grated Parmesan cheese

2 tablespoons toasted pine nuts

Parmesan crisps or prosciutto crisps (optional)

Heat the oil in a Dutch oven or large, heavy-bottomed saucepan over medium-high heat. Add the onion and cook, stirring frequently, until the onion starts to soften, 3 to 4 minutes. Add the garlic and cook for 1 minute, or until fragrant. Add the cauliflower and salt and stir until everything is well combined. Pour in the stock and add the Parmesan rind. Bring to a simmer and cook for 15 minutes, or the until cauliflower is tender. Remove from the heat and stir in the grated cheese and the pine nuts. Transfer the soup to a blender or use an immersion blender to blend until smooth. Top with Parmesan crisps or prosciutto crisps, if desired.

Cannellini and Escarole Soup

If I'm at an Italian restaurant and they have a cannellini and escarole soup on the menu, I order it. I love the big slices of garlic, tender beans, and the slightly bitter greens. I like to have a piece of crusty bread with it and use the bread to soak up every last bit in the bowl.

YIELD
4 to 6 servings

TOTAL TIME
40 minutes

¼ cup (60 ml) extra-virgin olive oil, plus more for drizzling

1 yellow onion, diced

4 cloves garlic, sliced

¼ teaspoon crushed red pepper, or more to taste

½ teaspoon dried thyme

Kosher salt and cracked black pepper

1 bunch escarole, washed, dried, and roughly chopped

Two 15½-ounce (439 g) cans cannellini beans, drained and rinsed

4 cups (960 ml) chicken stock

1-inch (2.5 cm) piece Parmesan rind

Grated Parmesan cheese

Heat the oil in a large Dutch oven or heavy-bottomed saucepan over medium-high heat. Add the onion and cook for 7 to 8 minutes, or until very soft and browned on the edges. Stir in the garlic, crushed red pepper, thyme, ½ teaspoon salt, and ½ teaspoon pepper and cook for 1 minute, stirring constantly. Add the escarole and stir until the greens are wilted, then add the beans and stir until everything is coated in spices and vegetables. Pour in the stock and add the Parmesan rind. Bring soup to a boil, then reduce the heat to a simmer, cover, and cook for 30 minutes. Taste for seasoning, adding more salt, pepper, and crushed red pepper, if desired. To serve, drizzle with oil and sprinkle with grated cheese.

Harissa Butternut Squash Soup

YIELD

4 to 6 servings

TOTAL TIME

30 minutes

I was lucky enough to travel to Morocco back in 2010, and I fell in love with the food. At every meal, they would bring out a huge spread of different dips, vegetables, breads, and always harissa. I gravitate toward anything spicy, and I found myself spreading harissa on just about everything. It plays so nicely with the sweet butternut squash and the smoky cumin. A little dollop of yogurt and a sprinkle of fresh mint to garnish balances out the spice, and some crunchy chickpeas (you can buy them in the snack aisle or roast some at home) gives a little texture.

1 tablespoon olive oil

1 yellow onion, diced

1 tablespoon minced fresh ginger

2 cloves garlic, minced

2 tablespoons harissa, plus more for garnish if you like it spicy

1 teaspoon ground cumin

1 butternut squash, peeled, seeded, and cut into 1-inch (2.5 cm) pieces

2 teaspoons kosher salt

4 cups (960 ml) vegetable stock

Juice of ½ lemon

For garnish: crispy chickpeas, plain yogurt, and chopped fresh mint

Heat the oil in a Dutch oven or large, heavy-bottomed saucepan over medium-high heat. Add the onion and cook, stirring frequently, until the onion starts to soften, 3 to 4 minutes. Add the ginger, garlic, harissa, and cumin and cook for 1 minute, or until very fragrant. Add the squash and salt and stir until everything is fully coated in the spice mixture. Pour in the stock. Bring to a simmer and cook for 15 minutes, or until the squash is tender. Remove from the heat and stir in the lemon juice. Transfer the soup to a blender or use an immersion blender to blend until smooth. Top with crispy chickpeas, a dollop of yogurt, and mint. Serve with additional harissa for extra spice.

White Chicken Chili

The first time I made this chicken chili, I couldn't stop eating it. I even woke up the next morning and had it for breakfast. I am a leftovers fan, but I took this chili to the next level. Pretty much had it for every meal until it was gone. The flavor is addictive and I also really like the texture of having both the ground chicken and shredded chicken, plus those creamy beans.

YIELD
4 to 6 servings

TOTAL TIME
1 hour
50 minutes

2 tablespoons olive oil

1 pound (455 g) ground chicken

1 large onion, diced

1 jalapeño, minced (seeds and membranes removed for less heat, if desired)

2 cloves garlic, minced

1 teaspoon ground cumin

1 teaspoon ground coriander

4 cups (960 ml) low-sodium chicken broth

2 cooked chicken breasts, shredded

1 cup (240 ml) salsa verde

2 teaspoons kosher salt

½ teaspoon freshly ground black pepper

Two 15½-ounce (439 g) cans cannellini beans, drained and rinsed

½ cup (120 ml) half-and-half

For garnish: tortilla chips, shredded cheese, sour cream, fresh cilantro, and scallions

Heat 1 tablespoon of the oil in a Dutch oven over medium-high heat. Add the ground chicken and use a wooden spoon to break up the meat as it browns. Remove chicken to a plate and set aside.

Add the remaining 1 tablespoon oil to the pot and reduce the heat to medium. Add the onion and jalapeño. Cook, stirring often, until the onion is translucent and tender, 5 to 6 minutes. Stir in the garlic, cumin, and coriander and cook until the spices are fragrant, 1 to 2 minutes. Add the broth, shredded chicken, cooked ground chicken, salsa verde, salt, and black pepper and use a wooden spoon to scrape up any browned bits on the bottom of the pan. Bring to a low boil, reduce the heat to a simmer, and cook, stirring occasionally, for 1 hour.

Stir in the beans and half-and-half and continue to simmer, uncovered, until the liquid has reduced and the chili is thick, about 30 minutes. Serve topped with tortilla chips, cheese, sour cream, cilantro, and scallions.

Classic Chicken Noodle Soup

YIELD
4 to 6 servings

TOTAL TIME
1 hour

What is more comforting than a bowl of homemade chicken noodle soup? Not much I can think of. When cold and flu season rolls around, make a big pot of this, let it cool completely, then freeze it in individual portions. You'll want to warm up bowls of this even when you're perfectly healthy, just because you want to feel warm and cozy to the core.

1 tablespoon olive oil

2 bone-in, skin-on chicken breasts

Kosher salt and freshly ground black pepper

1 large yellow onion, diced

3 large carrots, peeled, cut in half lengthwise, and sliced ¼ inch (6 mm) thick

3 celery stalks, sliced ¼ inch (6 mm) thick

2 quarts (2 L) low-sodium chicken broth

1 bay leaf

A few sprigs fresh thyme

8 ounces (225 g) egg noodles

2 tablespoons chopped fresh flat-leaf parsley

Heat the oil in a medium Dutch oven or stockpot over medium-high heat. Season the chicken on both sides with salt and pepper. Add the chicken to the pot, skin-side down, and cook until browned, 3 to 4 minutes. Flip and cook for another 2 minutes. Remove from the pot and add the onion, carrots, and celery to the pot. Sauté for 2 minutes, using a wooden spoon to scrape up any browned bits on the bottom of the pan. Season with 2 teaspoons salt and ¼ teaspoon pepper.

Pour in the broth, then return the chicken to the pot and add the bay leaf and thyme. Bring to a low boil, then reduce the heat to low. If a foam forms, skim off the top and discard. Cover and let simmer for 25 minutes.

Remove the chicken. Remove and discard skin and bones. Shred the meat with a fork and add back to the pot, along with the noodles. Bring to a low boil and cook until the noodles are just done, about 8 minutes. Stir in the parsley and serve.

Creamy Spinach Artichoke Pasta
76

Roasted Chicken with Croutons
81

Porterhouse Steak in an Iron Skillet
82

Spicy Buttermilk Grilled Chicken
85

Ryan's Ribs—Hoisin Style
86

Penne Pie
88

Prime Rib with Beef Gravy
91

Beef Stroganoff
92

Pork Chops with White Beans, Fennel, and Onions
95

Turkey Meatloaf
96

BBQ Potato Chip–Crusted Salmon with Peach Salsa
99

Quick Chicken Cutlet Saltimbocca
100

Skillet Broiled Shrimp
103

Sticky Soy-Ginger-Garlic Chicken Thighs
104

Maple-Sage Roasted Turkey in 8 Pieces
107

Croque Monsieur
108

Animal-Style Burgers
111

Spaghetti with Clams
112

Veggie Chili Cornbread Pot Pie
115

Apricot-Glazed Ham
117

Mushroom Bolognese with Rigatoni
119

Eggplant "Meat"Ball Sandwiches
120

Cheat Sheet Sausage, Peppers, and Onions with Polenta
123

Spaghetti with Zucchini
124

Easy Cast-Iron Skillet Pizza
127

Women's Club Chicken Legs
128

Grilled Red Curry Lamb Chops
131

Lemon Pasta
132

Caramelized Onion Burgers
135

Surf-and-Turf Skewers with Spicy Bourbon BBQ Sauce
137

Grilled Farmers' Market "Paella"
138

chapter three

———

ENTRÉES

Creamy Spinach Artichoke Pasta

YIELD
4 servings

TOTAL TIME
20 minutes

Real talk: I can destroy an order of spinach artichoke dip in mere minutes. Ryan and I got to talking and thought, *Why not make it pasta?* This is a total pantry/freezer/fridge recipe—frozen spinach, jarred artichoke hearts, cream cheese—and comes together really quickly. And we all know the best part of the spinach artichoke dip is the layer of melted cheese on the top . . . so of course, I went there.

1 pound (455 g) rigatoni (or any short pasta)

1 tablespoon extra-virgin olive oil

2 cloves garlic, minced

Pinch of crushed red pepper

One 10-ounce (283 g) package frozen spinach, cooked and drained

Half of an 8½-ounce (240 g) jar artichoke hearts, or about 4 ounces (115 g), drained and chopped

½ teaspoon dried basil

4 ounces (115 g) cream cheese, cubed

½ cup (50 g) finely grated Parmesan cheese

1½ cups (170 g) shredded mozzarella cheese

Kosher salt and freshly ground black pepper

Preheat the broiler.

Bring a large pot of water to a boil. Season aggressively with salt. Add the rigatoni and cook until al dente, about 2 minutes less than the package directions. Drain and reserve 2½ cups (600 ml) of the pasta water.

see front of book for correction

Roasted Chicken with Croutons

YIELD
4 servings

ACTIVE TIME
30 minutes

TOTAL TIME
2 hours (includes resting time)

If there is only one recipe you make from this entire cookbook, make it this one. I think this dish is the reason Ryan first fell in love with me. We were pretty early on in our relationship and we spent the day watching—what else—Nancy Meyers movies. We had a fire going and I had bought some Gruyère cheese bread from the local bakery, Breadzilla, and we drank Aperol Spritzes. That evening, I roasted this chicken with croutons. I served it with a simple bistro salad and a good bottle of red. It was pretty much the perfect day.

For the chicken and croutons:

One 4- to 5-pound (1.8 to 2.3 kg) roaster chicken

1 tablespoon kosher salt

1 teaspoon freshly ground black pepper

1 teaspoon garlic powder

6 sprigs fresh thyme

2 sprigs fresh rosemary

1 head garlic, sliced in half

½ yellow onion

1 baguette

3 tablespoons unsalted butter, at room temperature

Dijon mustard, for serving

For the bistro salad:

1 head Bibb lettuce, torn into bite-size pieces

Handful of chopped mixed fresh herbs, such as chives, tarragon, and parsley (about ¼ cup/13 g)

House Dressing (page 50)

Make the chicken and croutons: Preheat the oven to 425°F (220°C). When hot, put a cast-iron skillet in the oven to preheat for about 5 minutes.

Dry the chicken with paper towels. In a small bowl, mix together the salt, pepper, and garlic powder.

Generously season the chicken inside and out with the salt mixture. Stuff the chicken cavity with the thyme, rosemary, garlic, and onion.

Slice the baguette on the bias into five slices, each 2 inches (5 cm) thick. Spread some butter on one side of each slice. (Note: you may be tempted to use more than five slices, because you will have room for more. Resist the urge, because you want the bread to become fully soaked with the juice of the chicken. More slices and there won't be enough juices, leaving you with rather lackluster croutons.) Carefully remove the hot skillet from the oven and arrange the baguette slices buttered side down in the center of the skillet. Place the chicken on the baguette slices, making sure all of the bread is covered by the chicken. Roast until the chicken is golden brown, an instant-read thermometer reads 165°F (74°C), and the juices run clear, about 1 hour 15 minutes. Transfer the chicken to a cutting board and tent with foil. Let rest for 10 minutes before carving. Remove the baguette slices from the skillet and set aside.

Make the bistro salad: Combine the lettuce and herbs in a medium bowl. Toss with dressing to taste. Carve the chicken and serve with the baguette slices, mustard, and salad.

Porterhouse Steak in an Iron Skillet

YIELD
2 to 4 servings

ACTIVE TIME
15 minutes

TOTAL TIME
45 minutes
(includes resting time)

Once you make this recipe, you will never make a porterhouse steak any other way. When you read the technique, you're going to think I'm crazy. But you should know that none other than Bobby Flay taught me this method, and it *works*. Every. Single. Time. There is no point in going to a restaurant and spending steakhouse prices when you can make a steak this good, this easily, at home. Use a timer, follow the instructions exactly, and you'll never be disappointed.

1 porterhouse steak, 2 to 2½ inches (5 to 6 cm) thick

Kosher salt and freshly ground black pepper

1 tablespoon canola oil

2 tablespoons unsalted butter, cubed

Optional additions: garlic cloves and fresh thyme or rosemary sprigs

Let the steak rest at room temperature for 30 minutes.

Preheat the broiler. Heat a cast-iron skillet over medium-high heat until very hot. Season the steak heavily with salt and pepper on all sides. Add the oil to the skillet, then place the steak in the skillet and do not move it. Cook until a nice crust forms, about 3 minutes. Remove the skillet from the heat, transfer the steak to a cutting board, and cut both the filet and sirloin from the bone. Slice the steak against the grain into thick pieces. Put the bone back into the skillet and reassemble the steak around it (it should look like the steak originally did) with the seared side up. Top with the pieces of butter. Add a couple cloves of garlic and a few sprigs of thyme or rosemary, if desired.

Broil to desired doneness, about 4 minutes for medium-rare, 5 to 6 minutes for medium. Transfer to a serving plate and pour the pan drippings over the steak.

Spicy Buttermilk Grilled Chicken

YIELD
4 servings

ACTIVE TIME
30 minutes

TOTAL TIME
4 hours 30 minutes
(includes marinating
time)

Let's face it: Grilled chicken can be boring and D-R-Y. How many times have you had a grilled chicken breast and with one bite, every bit of moisture in your mouth has been sucked out? Spicy Buttermilk Grilled Chicken to the rescue! Bone-in chicken will always be juicier, and by soaking it in buttermilk first, it will be extra tender due to the acidity. I like just about everything spicy, so I add hot sauce to the mix. (This is basically the same soak I use when I make fried chicken: After the soak, I dredge it in flour, then lower it into the fryer.) If you like, serve this with homemade ranch dressing (page 49) and fresh herbs.

1 whole chicken, cut into 10 pieces

1 cup (240 ml) buttermilk

¼ cup (60 ml) hot sauce, preferably Frank's brand

1 teaspoon garlic powder

1 teaspoon onion powder

1 teaspoon paprika

Put the chicken in a bowl or resealable bag. Whisk the buttermilk and hot sauce together with the spices. Pour the marinade over the chicken and let sit in the refrigerator for at least 4 hours or up to overnight.

Preheat a grill pan or outdoor grill to medium-high. Remove the chicken from the marinade, shaking off any excess and discarding any leftover marinade. Place the chicken on the grill. Cover and cook for 8 to 10 minutes per side, until the chicken is fully cooked, the juices run clear when pierced, and the internal temperature reaches 165°F (74°C) on an instant-read thermometer. Transfer the chicken to a plate or cutting board and let rest for 5 to 10 minutes, then serve.

Ryan's Ribs— Hoisin Style

YIELD
4 servings

ACTIVE TIME
15 minutes

TOTAL TIME
3 hours 20 minutes

My husband makes the best ribs. His method involved seasoning them, then wrapping them tightly in aluminum foil and cooking at low temperature for a few hours. Then he bastes them with sauce and either puts them on the grill or under the broil to make them sticky and crispy. Use any kind of seasoning combo you like with his method (like classic BBQ spices and sauce) or try this version for hoisin ribs. It's hard to beat the combo of ginger, garlic, and hoisin.

For the ribs:

2 tablespoons grated fresh ginger

2 cloves garlic, grated

3 teaspoons kosher salt

½ teaspoon cracked black pepper

2 tablespoons vegetable oil

2 racks baby back ribs (about 4½ pounds/2 kg total)

For the sauce:

½ cup (120 ml) hoisin sauce

3 tablespoons soy sauce

3 tablespoons rice vinegar

2 tablespoons honey

1 tablespoon sesame oil

1 tablespoon grated fresh ginger

2 teaspoons sambal

1 clove garlic, grated

Make the ribs: Preheat the oven to 300°F (150°C).

Tear two sheets of aluminum foil (large enough to fully wrap each rack of ribs) and place on a work surface. Mix the ginger, garlic, salt, pepper, and oil in a small bowl. Rub the mixture all over the ribs. Place each rack on a piece of aluminum foil and tightly wrap. Place the foil-wrapped ribs on a rimmed baking sheet. Bake for 3 hours, or until the ribs are very tender.

In the meantime, make the sauce: In a small saucepan, combine all the ingredients over medium heat. Bring to a low simmer, then reduce the heat to low and cook for about 2 minutes. Remove from the heat.

Remove the ribs from the foil. Preheat the broiler or a grill to high. Use a knife to cut the ribs into pieces between the bones. In a bowl, toss the ribs with the sauce. Return the ribs to the baking sheet and broil for 3 to 5 minutes (or grill), until browned, bubbling, and crispy. Serve hot.

Penne Pie

YIELD
8 to 10 servings

ACTIVE TIME
30 minutes

TOTAL TIME
1 hour 5 minutes

Oh goodness, this is comfort in a springform pan. There is something so homey about this dish; it just makes you feel loved. I also make it with spaghetti, and if you have a few boxes of pasta around with just a little bit in each box, mix them together. You can also substitute ground turkey for the beef, or make it vegetarian with some sautéed zucchini and squash or mushrooms.

Kosher salt

1 pound (455 g) penne rigate

1 pound (455 g) ground beef (85% lean)

Freshly ground black pepper

1 tablespoon olive oil

1 yellow onion, chopped

2 cups (480 ml) marinara sauce, homemade or store-bought (I like Rao's)

½ cup (120 ml) whole-milk ricotta

2 tablespoons minced fresh flat-leaf parsley

3 large eggs

½ cup (50 g) plus 2 tablespoons grated Parmesan cheese

1 cup (110 g) shredded mozzarella cheese

Special equipment: 9-inch (23 cm) springform pan, 3 inches (7.5 cm) deep

Preheat the oven to 350°F (175°C). Grease a 9-inch (23 cm) springform pan with cooking spray.

Bring a large pot of salted water to a boil. Add the penne and cook for 3 to 4 minutes less than the package recommends, so that it is very al dente. Drain and reserve ¼ cup (60 ml) of the pasta water.

In a large skillet over medium-high heat, brown the beef, 5 to 8 minutes; season with salt and pepper.

Transfer the beef to a paper towel–lined plate to drain. Wipe the skillet clean with a paper towel. Heat the oil in the skillet over medium heat, add the onion, and sauté until translucent, 4 to 5 minutes. Set aside.

In a large bowl, whisk together the marinara, reserved pasta water, the ricotta, parsley, eggs, ½ cup (50 g) of the Parmesan, 1 teaspoon salt, and ¼ teaspoon pepper. Add the cooked penne, beef, and onions and toss to evenly coat. Transfer to the prepared pan, top with the mozzarella, and sprinkle with the remaining 2 tablespoons Parmesan.

Bake until the cheese is bubbling and golden brown, 25 to 30 minutes. Let rest for 5 minutes, then remove the sides of the pan, cut into wedges, and serve.

Prime Rib with Beef Gravy

YIELD

6 to 8 servings

ACTIVE TIME

30 minutes

TOTAL TIME

3 hours 15 minutes
(includes standing time)

If there were ever a dish to ooh and ahh at, this would be the one. Prime rib is so impressive but so simple to make it almost feels wrong. You can easily adapt this recipe for a larger cut of meat, if you like: Just add an additional 15 minutes of roasting time per pound. I once made a 20-pound (9 kg) prime rib for Christmas Eve dinner and it was nothing short of sensational. The gravy is optional; you can also serve the beef with horseradish.

One 6- to 7-pound (2.7 to 3.2 kg) bone-in prime rib (to make slicing easy, ask your butcher to cut the bones from the meat, then tie them back onto the roast)

3 cloves garlic, sliced

¼ cup (35 g) kosher salt

2 tablespoons coarsely ground black pepper

¼ cup (30 g) all-purpose flour

3 cups (720 ml) low-sodium beef stock

1 tablespoon Dijon mustard

A few sprigs fresh thyme

A few sprigs fresh rosemary

1 clove garlic, smashed

1 tablespoon sherry vinegar or red wine vinegar

Use the tip of a knife to make slits in the fat of the prime rib and stuff them with slices of garlic. In a small bowl, mix the salt and pepper. Create a crust of salt and pepper all over the meat. Let stand at room temperature for 30 minutes.

Preheat the oven to 450°F (230°C).

Put the prime rib on a rack in a roasting pan. Roast the meat for 10 minutes, then turn the oven temperature down to 350°F (175°C). Roast until the meat registers 120°F (49°C) on an instant-read thermometer for medium-rare, 1 hour 30 minutes to 1 hour 45 minutes (about 15 minutes per pound). Remove the meat to a cutting board, loosely tent with foil, and let stand for 20 minutes.

In the meantime, pour off most of the fat from the roasting pan, leaving a few tablespoons. Put the roasting pan on top of the stove over medium heat. Whisk the flour into the fat and cook for 2 to 3 minutes, to cook out the taste of the raw flour. Vigorously whisk in the stock and mustard. Add the thyme, rosemary, and garlic. Bring to a low boil, then reduce the heat to a simmer and cook, whisking, until the mixture begins to thicken. Add the vinegar and cook for 1 more minute. Transfer to a serving dish.

Remove the ties from the prime rib. Slice the prime rib and bones and serve with the gravy.

Beef Stroganoff

YIELD
8 servings

ACTIVE TIME
30 minutes

TOTAL TIME
2 hours 15 minutes

When I was twelve years old, we had a big snowstorm, and I decided that night I would host my first "dinner party." My mom and I walked to the grocery store in the snow and I got all of the ingredients to make beef stroganoff. I set the table and had her film me giving instructions for cooking the dish. My grandparents lived next door, so they came over to be my "party guests." The meal was a big success, and I guess the path to my future was cemented!

¼ teaspoon garlic powder

Kosher salt and cracked black pepper

2 pounds (910 g) chuck roast, cubed

⅓ cup (40 g) plus 3 tablespoons all-purpose flour

2 tablespoons canola oil

1 large yellow onion, sliced

¼ cup (60 ml) Cognac or dry sherry

3 cups (720 ml) low-sodium beef broth

1 tablespoon unsalted butter

8 ounces (225 g) cremini mushrooms, sliced

½ cup (120 ml) sour cream

1 pound (455 g) egg noodles, cooked, buttered, and seasoned

3 tablespoons chopped fresh chives

In a large bowl, mix the garlic powder with 1½ teaspoons salt and ¼ teaspoon pepper. Pat the beef dry with paper towels and add to the bowl; toss to coat. Add ⅓ cup (40 g) of the flour and toss again.

In a Dutch oven, heat the oil over medium-high heat. Working in batches, add the beef and cook until browned on all sides, about 5 minutes per batch. Transfer to a plate. Reduce the heat to medium and add the onion to the pot. Cook, stirring often, until fragrant and starting to soften, about 2 minutes. Add the Cognac and cook, scraping up any browned bits with a spoon, about 1 minute. Return the meat to the pot and add the broth. Bring to a simmer, then reduce the heat to low, cover, and simmer, stirring occasionally, until the beef is almost tender, about 1½ hours.

Transfer 1 cup (240 ml) of the broth from the pot to a small bowl; add the remaining 3 tablespoons flour and whisk until smooth. Add the flour mixture to the pot. Season to taste.

In a large skillet, melt the butter over medium heat. Add the mushrooms and cook, stirring often, until golden brown, 5 to 7 minutes. Add the mushrooms to the meat mixture. Simmer until the meat is tender, about 30 minutes longer.

Stir in the sour cream and season with salt and pepper. Place the noodles in a large bowl; spoon the beef over. Garnish with the chives and serve.

Pork Chops with White Beans, Fennel, and Onions

Ryan loves pork chops, but I hardly ever think to make them. I'm not really sure why, because they are so easy to cook and make for a relatively quick yet super-satisfying meal. Both pounding the pork chops and doing a quick braise helps keep them from drying out. We both favor foods that lean to the Tuscan flavors because we both studied in Florence, so he was especially pleased when I came up with this recipe one evening. The white beans, fennel, and onions definitely say "Tuscany."

YIELD
4 servings

ACTIVE TIME
35 minutes

TOTAL TIME
45 minutes

4 bone-in pork chops, 1 inch (2.5 cm) thick

Kosher salt and freshly ground black pepper

2 tablespoons olive oil

1 yellow onion, thinly sliced

1 fennel bulb, thinly sliced, fronds reserved for garnish

2 cloves garlic, thinly sliced

One 15½-ounce (439 g) can cannellini beans, drained and rinsed

½ cup (120 ml) white wine

1 teaspoon brown sugar

Place the pork chops one at a time between two sheets of parchment paper. Use a meat mallet to pound the pork chops to about ½ inch thick. Generously season each side of the pork chops with salt and pepper.

Heat the oil in a large skillet over medium-high heat. Add the pork chops and cook for about 3 minutes per side; remove and set aside. Add the onion and fennel to the pan and reduce the heat to medium. Cook until translucent and tender, 7 to 8 minutes. Add the garlic and beans and cook for 1 minute. Season with 1 teaspoon salt and ¼ teaspoon pepper. Stir in the wine and brown sugar, then return the chops to the skillet. Reduce the temperature to low, cover, and cook for 5 minutes.

Serve the chops with the onion, fennel, and beans spooned on top and garnished with fennel fronds.

Turkey Meatloaf

YIELD
6 to 8 servings

ACTIVE TIME
30 minutes

TOTAL TIME
1½ to 2 hours

We are big fans of meatloaf in our household. I used to call meatloaf "manloaf," because if you make it for a man, he will fall in love with you, but now I just call it "loveloaf," because anyone you make it for will feel the love. I actually enjoy making meatloaf when we have people for dinner, because it is so unexpected and universally enjoyed. I always serve it with mashed potatoes and green beans. And can anybody tell me anything that is better than leftover meatloaf the next day on white bread with mayo? Nope, because nothing is better.

1 tablespoon olive oil

½ yellow onion, diced

1 bay leaf

1 clove garlic, minced

1 red bell pepper, finely diced

2 tablespoons chopped fresh flat-leaf parsley

2 teaspoons chopped fresh thyme

2 pounds (910 g) ground dark meat turkey; or 1 pound ground turkey breast, 1 pound ground dark meat

2 large eggs, lightly beaten

¾ cup (75 g) dry breadcrumbs

1 tablespoon Worcestershire sauce

2 teaspoons kosher salt

½ teaspoon freshly ground black pepper

1 cup (240 ml) ketchup

Preheat the oven to 350°F (175°C). Line a baking sheet with parchment paper, then spray lightly with nonstick cooking spray.

Heat the oil in a medium skillet over medium heat. Add the onion and cook, stirring often, until translucent, 7 to 8 minutes. Add the bay leaf, garlic, bell pepper, parsley, and thyme. Cook, stirring often, until tender, about 5 minutes. Remove from the heat and let the mixture cool. Remove and discard the bay leaf.

In a large bowl, combine the turkey, eggs, breadcrumbs, Worcestershire sauce, cooled vegetables, salt, black pepper, and ½ cup (120 ml) of the ketchup. Use your hands to mix everything together until just combined. Take care not to overmix, as this will result in a tough meatloaf. Transfer the mixture to the center of the prepared baking sheet and form into a loaf. Coat the meatloaf in the remaining ½ cup (120 ml) ketchup. Bake until the meatloaf is firm and cooked through, 1 to 1½ hours. Let stand for 5 minutes before slicing and serving.

BBQ Potato Chip–Crusted Salmon with Peach Salsa

Salmon is my go-to for dinner parties. I buy a big piece of it and cook it whole, then serve it right on the pan and let everyone cut their own portion. For the longest time, I would season it with only chili powder and brown sugar, but I must've been feeling wild one day and decided to upgrade it with a crushed BBQ chip coating. I love the crunch that the chips add and the extra bit of tang that the BBQ sauce lends. The ripe peach salsa makes it totally next level. If you're making it in the winter or don't have access to ripe peaches, try it with mango instead.

YIELD
4 servings

ACTIVE TIME
15 minutes

TOTAL TIME
30 minutes

For the salmon:

1½ pounds (680 g) skin-on center-cut salmon fillet

Kosher salt and freshly ground black pepper

2 tablespoons BBQ sauce

1 cup (135 g) crushed BBQ potato chips

¼ cup (55 g) packed dark brown sugar

1 tablespoon chili powder

6 scallions, white and light green parts, chopped

1 clove garlic

Zest of 1 lime (reserve the juice for the salsa)

For the salsa:

3 ripe yellow peaches, finely diced

½ red onion, finely diced

½ jalapeño, minced

¼ cup (10 g) minced fresh cilantro

Juice of ½ lime

Salt and freshly ground black pepper

Make the salmon: Preheat the oven to 450°F (230°C). Line a baking sheet with parchment paper.

Place the salmon in the center of the prepared baking sheet, skin side down. Season with 1 teaspoon salt and ½ teaspoon pepper. Spread the BBQ sauce evenly on the flesh side of the salmon.

In a food processor, combine the BBQ chips, brown sugar, chili powder, scallions, garlic, and lime zest and pulse until combined and the consistency of coarse breadcrumbs. Press the mixture onto the sauce on the flesh side of the salmon.

Bake until the chip mixture is golden brown and crunchy, about 15 minutes.

Meanwhile, make the salsa: In a medium bowl, combine all the ingredients, seasoning with salt and pepper to taste.

Serve the salmon with the salsa.

Quick Chicken Cutlet Saltimbocca

YIELD
4 servings

ACTIVE TIME
10 minutes

TOTAL TIME
15 minutes

Saltimbocca is an Italian dish of either thinly pounded chicken or veal that is marinated in sage then baked with cheese and prosciutto. To get the same great flavor but without taking the time to pound out chicken breasts, marinate them, and bake them, I came up with this hack, which requires considerably less effort.

4 boneless, skinless thin-sliced chicken breasts

Kosher salt and freshly ground black pepper

4 fresh sage leaves

4 slices prosciutto

1 tablespoon olive oil

4 slices provolone cheese

Preheat the oven to 400°F (205°C). Tear off four pieces of parchment paper, each slightly larger than one chicken breast slice.

Place each chicken breast on a piece of the parchment paper. Season with salt and pepper. Top each with a sage leaf and a slice of prosciutto.

Heat the oil in a large ovenproof skillet over medium-high heat. Pick up each chicken breast by the parchment paper and slap it prosciutto slice down into the skillet. Remove the paper. Cook until the prosciutto is crisp, about 3 minutes. Use a spatula to flip the chicken breasts, then top each with a slice of cheese. Transfer the skillet to the oven. Bake for 4 to 5 minutes, until the chicken is cooked through and the cheese is melted and bubbly. (If you want the cheese to brown more, turn on the broiler for 1 to 2 minutes.) Serve hot.

Skillet Broiled Shrimp

YIELD
4 servings

TOTAL TIME
10 minutes

This wins the prize for your fastest dinner ever—5 minutes! How about that? The best thing about shrimp is that it cooks so quickly; the worst thing about shrimp is that it cooks so quickly. It is really easy to overcook shrimp, taking it from delicate, sweet, and delicious to rubbery, chewy, and dry. If you're at all intimidated, get out your phone and set your timer. I promise you that it will not be undercooked. Remember, carry-over cooking is real, so even if you think it's the slightest bit underdone (it won't be), it's going to be *prime* eating by the time it gets to your plate. Round out the meal with a salad and a piece of crusty baguette to soak up all that garlicky goodness in the skillet!

4 tablespoons (55 g) unsalted butter

3 cloves garlic, minced

2 shallots, minced

Pinch of crushed red pepper

2 pounds (910 g) large shrimp, peeled and deveined

Crusty bread, for serving

Preheat the broiler to high.

In a large ovenproof skillet over medium heat, melt the butter with the garlic, shallots, and crushed red pepper for about 2 minutes. Remove from the heat. Toss in the shrimp. Place the skillet under the broiler for about 3 minutes, until the shrimp is opaque and just begins to curl up. Serve immediately with crusty bread to dip in the pan juices.

Sticky Soy-Ginger-Garlic Chicken Thighs

The other day, I asked Ryan what his favorite thing that I make is. He looked at me quizzically and said, "Is this a trick question?" I assured him it was not, and this chicken thigh dish was his response. I wasn't that surprised, though, because he is addicted to the flavors of ginger and garlic, and he loves anything with fish sauce. The amounts of garlic and ginger in this recipe may seem a bit aggressive, but trust me: They are warranted. Be sure to serve this with a bowl of white rice because you will want it to soak up every last bit of the sauce.

YIELD
4 servings

ACTIVE TIME
35 minutes

TOTAL TIME
55 minutes

8 skin-on, bone-in chicken thighs

Kosher salt and freshly ground black pepper

2 tablespoons unsalted butter

½ cup (110 g) packed dark brown sugar

8 cloves garlic, finely minced

2-inch (5 cm) piece fresh ginger, finely minced

⅓ cup (75 ml) rice vinegar

¼ cup (60 ml) fish sauce

¼ cup (60 ml) low-sodium soy sauce

1 tablespoon coconut or vegetable oil

White rice, for serving

Preheat the oven to 400°F (205°C).

Use a paper towel to thoroughly dry the chicken thighs. Season both sides with salt and pepper. Set aside.

Melt the butter in a small saucepan over medium-high heat. Add the brown sugar and cook, stirring constantly, until it begins to melt, 2 to 3 minutes. Add the garlic and ginger and cook, continuing to stir, for another 1 to 2 minutes, until very fragrant. Stir in the vinegar, fish sauce, and soy sauce. Bring to a low simmer and cook for about 5 minutes. Remove from the heat.

Heat a large ovenproof skillet over high heat until very hot. Add the coconut oil. Place the chicken in the skillet skin side down and let brown without moving it for about 4 minutes (do not overcrowd the pan; if necessary, cook the chicken in two batches). Remove the chicken to a plate and drain off all but about 1 tablespoon of the fat. Return the skillet to medium-high heat and add the brown sugar mixture. Use a wooden spoon to scrape up any browned bits. Return the chicken to the skillet, skin side up. Spoon the sauce over the chicken. Transfer the skillet to the oven and bake, basting the chicken with the sauce midway through cooking, until cooked through, about 20 minutes. Turn the oven to broil and broil until the skin is extra-crispy and browned, 2 to 3 minutes. Serve over white rice with the sauce.

Maple-Sage Roasted Turkey in 8 Pieces

YIELD

6 to 8 servings

ACTIVE TIME

15 to 20 minutes

TOTAL TIME

2 hours 30 minutes
to 3 hours

I've made my Thanksgiving turkey pretty much exactly the same way every year. I dry brine, stuff an herb butter under the skin, and baste with a mixture of stock with a little maple syrup (which adds color and flavor). I've always liked that Norman Rockwell moment of the turkey coming to the table on a platter in all of its glory. But let's be honest, the glory ends there. It's a pain to carve. I decided to try cooking it in parts. I asked the butcher to cut it up for me (my mom told me her grocery store didn't have a butcher and I explained to her that's who the people in white lab coats behind the meat counter are), then I used my usual flavor profile, and roasted it in—get this—an hour and fifteen minutes. Super simple, no drama of the breast getting done before the thigh, and no muss, no fuss in the carving department.

One 12- to 14-pound (5.4 to 6.4 kg) turkey, cut into 8 pieces

½ cup (1 stick/115 g) unsalted butter

¼ cup (60 ml) maple syrup

2 teaspoons garlic powder

2 teaspoons onion powder

2 teaspoons dried sage

1 tablespoon kosher salt

Freshly ground black pepper

Preheat the oven to 400°F (205°C). Line two rimmed baking sheets with parchment paper (which definitely makes cleanup easier) and place a wire rack on each sheet (I use wire cooling racks).

In a small saucepan, combine the butter, maple syrup, garlic powder, onion powder, and sage over medium heat. Whisk until the butter is completely melted and the ingredients are well combined.

In a large bowl, toss the turkey parts with the melted butter mixture. Transfer to the prepared baking racks in a single layer. Season both sides of each turkey piece with salt and pepper.

Roast until golden brown and an instant-read thermometer reads 165°F (74°C), about 1 hour 15 minutes.

Let the turkey rest for 30 to 40 minutes before slicing the meat and serving the pieces.

Croque Monsieur

YIELD
6 servings

ACTIVE TIME
35 minutes

TOTAL TIME
35 minutes

When I go to Paris, I always plan a lunch at Café Flore on the Left Bank. I like to sit at a table outside. I order a croque monsieur and a glass of wine and watch the world go by. They may sound a bit daunting to make at home, but you can actually make the sauce ahead of time, then assemble the sandwiches on a baking sheet and do them all at once. It's actually a really fun dish to serve for a dinner party because it is so unexpected. If you've made my baked ham (page 117) for Christmas or Easter, this is a great way to use up the leftovers, especially if you have a house full of family for the holidays.

12 slices white sandwich bread

Dijon mustard

Sliced ham, as needed, depending on how thick your ham is (if using thinly sliced deli ham, use about 3 slices per sandwich, if using leftover Apricot-Glazed Ham, page 117, 1 or 2 slices)

4 cups (450 g) shredded Gruyère cheese

3 tablespoons unsalted butter

¼ cup (30 g) all-purpose flour

2 cups (480 ml) whole milk

Pinch of grated nutmeg

Kosher salt and freshly ground black pepper

Preheat the oven to 400°F (205°C).

Assemble the sandwiches on a baking sheet by spreading 6 slices of bread with a scant amount of mustard. (If you like more Dijon flavor, add more; I like it to be subtle.) Top with the ham and sprinkle each sandwich with about 1 tablespoon of the cheese. Top with the remaining bread slices.

In a medium saucepan, heat the butter over medium heat until melted. Stir in the flour, creating a roux, and cook for about 4 minutes. Whisk in the milk and stir until it thickens enough to coat the back of a spoon, about 5 to 6 minutes. Add the nutmeg and 1 cup of the cheese, and season with salt and pepper. Pour the mixture over the sandwiches. Top the sandwiches with the remaining cheese.

Bake for 8 minutes. Turn on the broiler and broil until the sandwiches are golden brown and the cheese is bubbly, about 2 minutes (watch closely!). Serve hot.

Animal-Style Burgers

YIELD
4 servings

ACTIVE TIME
35 minutes

TOTAL TIME
55 minutes
(includes chilling
time)

If you've ever been to California, chances are you've eaten at In-N-Out Burger. The line is always around the block and for good reason. Their burger is pretty much exactly how I like mine—not too thick, just the right patty-to-bun ratio—and they use American cheese. The not-so-secret menu includes "animal-style" burgers, which have caramelized onions and extra sauce. But did you know that part of the animal-style secret is to put yellow mustard on the patty *before* it is put on the griddle? Yep, makes all the difference. No need to wait in line for the burgers now, you can just make them at home!

1 onion, ½ grated, ½ thinly sliced

1 clove garlic, grated

1 large egg

1 teaspoon kosher salt

¼ teaspoon freshly ground black pepper

1 pound (455 g) ground beef (80% lean)

1 tablespoon unsalted butter

3 tablespoons yellow mustard

8 slices American cheese

Special Sauce (recipe follows)

4 potato buns, buttered and lightly toasted

Iceberg lettuce

Sliced tomato

Pickles

Spray a baking sheet with nonstick cooking spray. In a medium bowl, whisk together the grated onion, garlic, egg, salt, and pepper. Add the ground beef and use your hands to gently mix until combined. Divide the mixture evenly into four portions, then divide each into two, to give you eight total. Form each into a thin patty and place on the prepared baking sheet. The mixture will be wet and a bit sticky. Refrigerate for 20 minutes.

Heat a griddle or large cast-iron skillet over medium-high heat. Add the butter and sliced onion and cook, stirring every so often, until the onion slices have a nice sear to them, 4 to 5 minutes. Set aside.

Wipe the griddle clean and return to medium-high heat. Put the patties on the griddle, working in batches if necessary. Spoon about 1 teaspoon mustard (or squeeze directly from the bottle) onto the top raw side of each patty. Cook for about 3 minutes, then flip and cook for an additional 3 minutes. Top each with a slice of American cheese.

Spread some Special Sauce on each bottom bun, then add lettuce, one patty, some onions, a second patty, tomatoes, pickles, more sauce, and a top bun. Serve.

Special Sauce
YIELD: ABOUT 1 CUP (240 ML)

½ cup (120 ml) mayonnaise

3 tablespoons yellow mustard

2 tablespoons sweet relish

1 tablespoon ketchup

1 tablespoon apple cider vinegar

1 teaspoon garlic powder

1 teaspoon onion powder

1 teaspoon paprika

Combine all the ingredients in a medium bowl and whisk until well blended.

Spaghetti with Clams

YIELD
4 servings

ACTIVE TIME
25 minutes

TOTAL TIME
25 minutes

Last summer in the Hamptons, Ryan and I got on a big spaghetti with clams kick. The littleneck clams come from the waters just outside our back door, and they are so incredibly fresh tasting. I started making a toasted garlic breadcrumb mixture to garnish the pasta, and that's when we became obsessed. It was exactly what the dish needed! Every time I make it, I want to put on a cream turtleneck and pretend I'm Diane Keaton in *Something's Gotta Give*, when she makes it for Jack Nicholson.

For the breadcrumbs:

1 tablespoon unsalted butter

2 teaspoons extra-virgin olive oil

¼ teaspoon garlic salt

1 cup (80 g) panko breadcrumbs

1 teaspoon minced fresh parsley

For the pasta:

Kosher salt

1 pound (455 g) spaghetti

3 tablespoons extra-virgin olive oil, plus more for drizzling

3 cloves garlic, thinly sliced

Pinch of crushed red pepper

⅓ cup (75 ml) dry white wine

3 dozen littleneck clams, scrubbed clean

2 tablespoons unsalted butter

¼ cup (13 g) minced fresh flat-leaf parsley

Make the breadcrumbs: In a medium skillet over medium heat, melt the butter with the oil. Add the garlic salt. Stir in the breadcrumbs and toss to coat.

Increase the heat to medium-high and cook until the breadcrumbs are just toasted golden brown. Remove from the heat and stir in the parsley.

Make the pasta: Bring a large pot of water to a boil. Season aggressively with salt. Cook the pasta until al dente (I usually do about 2 minutes less than the package directions). Drain, reserving 1 cup (240 ml) of the pasta water; do not rinse.

Combine the oil and garlic in a large skillet, then place the skillet over medium heat. (I put oil and garlic in a room-temperature skillet and then bring to heat to keep the garlic from burning.) Cook for 1 to 2 minutes, stirring constantly so that the garlic does not burn. Add the crushed red pepper. Stir in the wine and about ¼ cup (60 ml) of the pasta water. Bring to a low simmer. Add the clams and cover the pan. Cook until all of the clams open, about 5 minutes (any clams that do not open are not good; throw them out). Stir in the butter and pasta, tossing to coat the pasta. Cook for about 1 minute. Stir in the parsley. Serve topped with the toasted breadcrumbs and a drizzle of oil.

Veggie Chili Cornbread Pot Pie

When I make a big pot of chili, I always make cornbread, so I figured, why not combine the two? This hearty veggie chili is packed with beans, butternut squash, and tomatoes. You can absolutely make a pot of it and stop there if you don't want to do a pot pie, or make the cornbread on its own in an iron skillet. I love them together, though, because when the chili is baked after it's simmered on the stove, the flavors get even more concentrated. Cilantro honey butter spread onto the hot cornbread? Yes, please!

YIELD
4 to 6 servings

TOTAL TIME
60 minutes

For the chili:

2 tablespoons extra-virgin olive oil

1 small butternut squash, peeled, seeded and diced (3½ cups/495 g)

1½ teaspoons kosher salt

1 yellow onion, diced

1 red bell pepper, diced

1 green bell pepper, diced

3 cloves garlic, minced

1 tablespoon chili powder

1 teaspoon dried oregano

½ teaspoon ground cumin

One 28-ounce (794 g) can whole peeled tomatoes, crushed by hand

One 16-ounce (453 g) jar salsa

One 15½-ounce (439 g) can black beans, drained and rinsed

One 15½-ounce (439 g) can pinto beans, drained and rinsed

2 cups (480 ml) vegetable stock

Freshly ground black pepper

For the cornbread:

1 cup (180 g) fine-ground yellow cornmeal

1 cup (125 g) all-purpose flour

1 tablespoon baking powder

2 tablespoons sugar

1 teaspoon kosher salt

1 cup (240 ml) buttermilk

2 tablespoons unsalted butter, melted

1½ cups (170 g) shredded cheddar cheese

1 large egg

For the cilantro honey butter:

2 tablespoons unsalted butter, softened

1 tablespoon minced fresh cilantro

2 teaspoons honey

Pinch of kosher salt

RECIPE CONTINUES

Make the chili: Heat the oil in a large, heavy-bottomed saucepan over medium-high heat. Add the squash and 1 teaspoon of the salt and sauté for about 5 minutes, until the squash starts to soften and brown. Add the onion and peppers and cook for about 5 minutes more, until the onion is soft. Stir in the garlic, chili powder, oregano, cumin, and the remaining ½ teaspoon salt and cook for 2 to 3 minutes more, until the spices are aromatic and the garlic is soft. Pour in the tomatoes and salsa, scraping up any browned bits on the bottom, and bring to a simmer. Add the beans and stock. Bring to a boil, then reduce the heat and simmer for 1 hour. Taste and season with salt and pepper.

Preheat the oven to 425°F (220°C).

While chili is simmering, make the cornbread mixture: Put all the cornbread ingredients in a large bowl and whisk until well combined.

Transfer the chili to a 9 by 13-inch (23 by 33 cm) baking dish and use a tablespoon or scoop to dollop the cornbread mixture on top. Bake for 25 to 30 minutes, until golden brown on top. Remove from the oven.

Make the cilantro honey butter: Mix all the ingredients together in a bowl. Spread the herb butter over the cornbread. Let stand for 5 minutes before serving.

Apricot-Glazed Ham

YIELD

8 to 10 servings

ACTIVE TIME

15 minutes

TOTAL TIME

2 hours 55 minutes

I make a ham twice a year, at Christmas and Easter. Generally, when it comes to holiday cooking, I don't change up my recipes. I have an idea of what that holiday is supposed to taste like and I don't like to stray from it. This is the way I always cook my ham. I think ham needs the sweetness that the apricot jam provides and I like the way the sugars caramelize and get slightly burned on the edges. And you gotta have mashed potatoes on the side, of course.

One 7- to 8-pound (3.2 to 3.6 kg) cured smoked ham, bone in

2 cups (480 ml) apricot jam

2 tablespoons unsalted butter, plus more for greasing the foil

2 tablespoons Dijon mustard

2 tablespoons minced fresh sage

1 tablespoon red wine vinegar

1 bay leaf

Pinch of ground cloves

Pinch of ground cinnamon

Preheat the oven to 375°F (190°C).

Place the ham on a roasting rack in a roasting pan with the fat side up. Use a knife to lightly score the fat in a diamond pattern, taking care not to cut into the meat. Bake the ham for 1 hour.

While the ham is baking, make the glaze: In a small saucepan, combine the jam, butter, mustard, sage, vinegar, bay leaf, cloves, and cinnamon over medium-low heat. Cook, stirring, until the glaze is thin and syrupy.

After the ham has baked for 1 hour, brush it with about half of the glaze and return to the oven.

Cook, brushing the ham with glaze every 15 to 20 minutes, until the internal temperature reaches about 130°F (54°C), 1 to 1½ hours longer. If the glaze starts to burn, tent with a piece of greased aluminum foil.

Remove the ham from the oven and tent with a piece of greased foil. Let rest for about 10 minutes, then carve and serve warm.

Mushroom Bolognese with Rigatoni

We try to go meatless a couple of days a week. Very often, dinner will just be a mix of whatever roasted vegetables I had in the fridge, some seared tofu, and a grain. Pasta is another go-to, and this mushroom Bolognese is one of the best options. For lack of a better word, it's just so "meaty." No one is going to eat this and say, "Where's the beef?" The mixture of mushrooms is bursting with flavor and texture, and the red wine adds depth. The heavy cream is optional, so if you want to make it lighter, you can leave it out.

YIELD
4 servings

ACTIVE TIME
30 minutes

TOTAL TIME
1 hour

1 carrot, cut into 1-inch (2.5 cm) pieces

8 ounces (225 g) white button mushrooms

8 ounces (225 g) cremini mushrooms

8 ounces (225 g) shiitake mushrooms

¼ cup (60 ml) extra-virgin olive oil

2 shallots, minced

2 cloves garlic, minced

5 tablespoons (75 ml) tomato paste

2 teaspoons kosher salt, plus more for the pasta water

¼ teaspoon freshly ground black pepper

½ cup (120 ml) red wine

½ cup (120 ml) heavy cream (optional)

1 pound (455 g) rigatoni

½ cup (50 g) finely grated Parmesan cheese

In a food processor, combine the carrot and all the mushrooms. Pulse until the mixture has the consistency of ground meat.

Heat the oil in a large deep skillet over medium heat. Add the shallots and garlic and cook, stirring constantly, for about 3 minutes, until the garlic is tender. Stir in the mushroom mixture. Increase the heat to medium-high and cook until the mushrooms begin to have some color and have released their water, 8 to 10 minutes. Stir in the tomato paste, salt, and pepper. Add the red wine and cream, if using. Reduce the heat to low, cover, and cook for 30 minutes.

Bring a large pot of water to a boil. Season aggressively with salt. Add the rigatoni and cook until al dente, about 2 minutes less than the package directions. Drain and reserve ½ cup (120 ml) of the pasta water. Stir the rigatoni into the mushroom sauce. Add about half of the pasta water, more if it seems dry. Cook for 1 to 2 minutes. Remove from the heat and stir in the cheese. Serve immediately.

Eggplant "Meat"Ball Sandwiches

YIELD
4 servings

ACTIVE TIME
40 minutes

TOTAL TIME
1 hour 25 minutes

I love a meatball. In my quest to add plant-based recipes to my diet, I tried making meatballs out of a mixture of eggplant and mushrooms, with great results. I like adding cashews for texture as well as a little protein. These meatball sandwiches taste really indulgent (hello, melted provolone!), but I also love using the eggplant balls on spaghetti with marinara. Even your pickiest meat eater will be very happy. Promise.

6 cups (490 g) diced eggplant, peel left on (about 1 medium eggplant)

2 tablespoons plus 1 teaspoon olive oil

Kosher salt and freshly ground black pepper

8 ounces (225 g) cremini mushrooms, quartered

½ cup (60 g) unsalted raw cashews

½ cup (40 g) panko breadcrumbs

¼ cup (25 g) grated Parmesan cheese, plus more for serving

2 cloves garlic, grated

2 tablespoons minced fresh flat-leaf parsley

1 large egg, lightly whisked

2 tablespoons unsalted butter, softened

4 kaiser rolls

1½ cups (360 ml) marinara sauce (your favorite store-bought or homemade)

4 slices provolone cheese

4 fresh basil leaves

Pickled banana peppers (optional)

Preheat the oven to 450°F (230°C). Line two baking sheets with parchment paper.

Put the eggplant in a large bowl and slowly drizzle with 1 tablespoon of the oil. Stir and drizzle in an additional tablespoon of oil. Sprinkle generously with salt and pepper and toss to combine. Spread out on a prepared baking sheet.

Combine the mushrooms and the remaining 1 teaspoon oil and spread on the second baking sheet. Bake the eggplant and mushrooms for 10 minutes, then stir and bake for an additional 10 minutes. (Reserve one baking sheet with parchment paper to use again to bake the meatballs.) Reduce the oven temperature to 400°F (205°C).

Pulse the eggplant a few times in a food processor until coarse in texture. Transfer to a large bowl. Pulse the mushrooms until coarse and add to the same bowl. Pulse the cashews until coarse and transfer to the bowl. (Processing everything together will make the mixture too mushy; be sure to take the time to process the ingredients one by one.) Add the breadcrumbs, Parmesan, garlic, parsley, egg, ½ teaspoon salt, and a little pepper. Stir to combine. Use an ice cream scoop or your hands to scoop the eggplant mixture into 12 balls and arrange them on the reserved lined baking sheet. Bake until crispy and browned, about 20 minutes.

Spread butter onto the kaiser rolls and toast in the oven until lightly golden brown. Toss the eggplant balls with marinara and place 3 on the bottom piece of each roll. Top with provolone and bake until the cheese melts, about 4 minutes. Remove from the oven and top each with a torn basil leaf and the top roll. Serve with banana peppers and grated Parmesan, if desired.

Cheat Sheet Sausage, Peppers, and Onions with Polenta

YIELD
4 servings

TOTAL TIME
35 minutes

Every September, the streets of Little Italy close to traffic and fill with stands serving up zeppoli, pizzas, cannoli, and, of course, sausage and peppers. Yes, it is very touristy and not quite as "nonna" as it used to be, but I still like to go and get a hoagie loaded with grilled Italian sausage, peppers, and onions. This cheat sheet is an easy way to get all of those flavors at home; a store-bought tube of polenta rounds out the meal with a starch. You could always just load it onto a roll with a slice of provolone melted on top, though, if you prefer!

1 pound (455 g) Italian sausage links

1 red onion, sliced

1 red bell pepper, sliced

1 yellow bell pepper, sliced

4 tablespoons (60 ml) extra-virgin olive oil

1 teaspoon garlic salt

Eight ½-inch (12 mm) slices polenta (about 8 ounces/225 g)

Kosher salt and cracked black pepper

3 tablespoons grated Parmesan cheese

Preheat the oven to 450°F (230°C).

Put the sausage, onion, and peppers on a rimmed baking sheet. Drizzle with 2 tablespoons of the oil and sprinkle with the garlic salt, tossing lightly with tongs to coat. Bake for 15 minutes.

Meanwhile, toss the polenta slices with the remaining 2 tablespoons oil and a pinch of salt and pepper. Remove the baking sheet from the oven and flip the sausage and vegetables. Add the polenta and return to the oven for another 15 minutes. Flip again. Turn the oven to broil. Sprinkle everything with cheese and broil for 2 to 3 minutes, until everything is brown and lightly charred.

Spaghetti with Zucchini

YIELD
4 servings

TOTAL TIME
10 minutes

Ryan and I got married in a restaurant on the Amalfi Coast called Lo Scoglio. In our opinion, it has the best food in the world. The family who owns it, the De Simones, grow all of the produce that they serve, and they harvest all of the restaurant's seafood themselves. The restaurant is run by the sisters Antonia and Margherita, and their brother Tommasso is the chef. Their father, Peppino, operates the farm. We go to see them every year, and they have become our Italian family. Lo Scoglio is famous for many things, but it's perhaps most well known for its spaghetti with zucchini. At our wedding at midnight, Antonia came to the dance floor with the biggest bowl of zucchini pasta I had ever seen. Everyone devoured it. I once asked her for the recipe and she obliged, but told me, "It will never taste the same, though, because you do not have our zucchini." She was right, but it's still pretty darn good.

Kosher salt

1 pound (455 g) spaghetti

6 tablespoons (90 ml) extra-virgin olive oil

1 clove garlic, smashed but left whole

3 zucchini, thinly sliced

12 fresh basil leaves, torn

½ cup (50 g) grated Parmesan cheese, plus more for serving if you'd like

½ cup (50 g) grated pecorino cheese

Bring a large pot of salted water to a boil. Add the spaghetti and cook until al dente, 9 to 11 minutes. Drain and reserve 1 cup (240 ml) of the pasta water.

Meanwhile, heat the oil in a large skillet over medium heat. Add the garlic; when it begins to sizzle, add the zucchini and sauté for a couple of minutes. Add ¼ cup (60 ml) of the pasta water and cook until the zucchini is tender, about 5 minutes. Add ¼ teaspoon salt and half of the basil. Remove and discard the garlic.

Add the pasta to the skillet along with about ½ cup (120 ml) of the reserved pasta water; shake the pan vigorously, adding a little more cooking water if the pasta looks dry. Cook, tossing, until the liquid is absorbed, 3 to 4 minutes. Remove from the heat and add the Parmesan, pecorino, and the remaining basil; toss. Top with more Parmesan, if desired, and serve.

Easy Cast-Iron Skillet Pizza

YIELD
4 to 6 servings

TOTAL TIME
30 minutes

I am certifiably pizza-obsessed. Several years ago, I went to a pizza school called Verace Pizza Napoletana, whose mission is to "defend the honor of Neapolitan pizza." To me, there is no pizza better than a Neapolitan pizza margherita. A thin, bubbly crust made of double-zero flour, simple tomato sauce, fresh mozzarella, a drizzle of extra-virgin olive oil, and fresh basil, cooked in 90 seconds in a 900°F (480°C) wood-burning pizza oven. My mouth is watering just thinking about it. Let's be honest, though, it's not realistic to make that kind of pizza at home very often, if at all. If you find yourself with a hankering for pizza, and you want to whip up a homemade version without waiting for dough to rise, *this* is the recipe for you. Homemade pizza dough with just two ingredients—Greek yogurt and self-rising flour—and no wait time for it to rise. It's food science at its best!

2 tablespoons extra-virgin oil

1 cup (240 ml) Greek yogurt

1 cup (125 g) self-rising flour

¼ teaspoon kosher salt

¼ cup (60 ml) pizza sauce (jarred or homemade)

4 ounces (115 g) low-moisture part-skim mozzarella, freshly grated

2 tablespoons grated Parmesan cheese

Preheat the oven to 425°F (220°C). Brush a 12-inch (30.5 cm) cast-iron skillet with 1 tablespoon of the oil.

Mix the yogurt, flour, and salt together with your hands until it becomes a ball, then flatten into a disk and press into the skillet. Spread the pizza sauce over the dough, leaving a 1-inch (2.5 cm) border around the sides, for the crust. Sprinkle the cheeses evenly over the sauce. Brush the crust with the remaining oil. Bake for 18 to 20 minutes, until bubbly and lightly browned, then let cool in the pan for 3 minutes. Carefully slide the pizza out onto a cutting board, slice, and serve.

Women's Club Chicken Legs

YIELD
4 to 6 servings

ACTIVE TIME
10 minutes

TOTAL TIME
45 minutes

Several years ago, I was lucky enough to get my grandma's old women's club cookbooks from the 1960s and '70s. It's so interesting to go through the recipes and see what was popular then, what they thought was new and exotic, and read my grandma's notes in the margins on what worked and what didn't. Some of the recipes sound like they should be left back in time (aspic!) and others have stood the test of time. I tried a chicken recipe that combined BBQ sauce and French dressing (the bottled orange kind, which I don't think I had purchased since the late 1990s), and it was *delicious*. I've spruced it up a bit with the addition of some vinegar and garlic, and I hope this is a recipe that my grandkids will make in decades to come.

12 chicken drumsticks (about 2¼ pounds/1 kg)

Kosher salt and freshly ground black pepper

½ cup (120 ml) BBQ sauce

½ cup (120 ml) French dressing

¼ cup (60 ml) red wine vinegar

2 cloves garlic, minced

2 tablespoons olive oil

Preheat the oven to 350°F (175°C). Line a rimmed baking sheet with parchment paper.

Use a paper towel to pat the chicken dry. Generously season on all sides with salt and pepper. In a large bowl, whisk together the BBQ sauce, dressing, vinegar, and garlic and set aside.

Heat the oil in a large skillet over medium-high heat. Add the chicken and cook for 2 to 3 minutes per side, until browned (you may need to do this in two batches).

Remove the chicken from the skillet to the bowl with the sauce. Toss to coat and place on the prepared baking sheet; reserve the extra marinade. Bake for 20 minutes, then remove the baking sheet from the oven and increase the oven temperature to 425°F (220°C). Spoon all of the reserved sauce over the chicken. Return to the oven and bake until the glaze on the skin is caramelized, about 15 minutes more.

Serve the chicken on a platter and pour any marinade from the baking sheet over it.

Grilled Red Curry Lamb Chops

YIELD
4 servings

ACTIVE TIME
15 minutes

TOTAL TIME
1 hour 35 minutes

This recipe gets a gold star from Ryan. I'm always trying to make food that is "crave-able," and this is one that he craves and requests on a regular basis. The marinade is super simple (three ingredients!), and lamb chops need only a few minutes on the grill, so it's a quick and easy dinner.

Zest and juice of 1 lime

½ cup (120 ml) coconut milk

3 tablespoons red curry paste

12 lamb chops

Kosher salt and freshly ground black pepper

Lime wedges and fresh cilantro leaves, for serving

In a large bowl, whisk the lime zest and juice, coconut milk, and curry paste. Add the lamb chops to the marinade and toss to coat. Cover and refrigerate for 1 hour. Remove from the refrigerator about 20 minutes before cooking. Remove the lamb from marinade and pat dry with a paper towel. Generously season on each side with salt and pepper.

Preheat an outdoor grill or grill pan to medium-high. Grill the lamb chops for 3 to 4 minutes, until slightly charred. Flip and cook for 2 to 3 minutes for medium doneness. Serve with lime wedges and cilantro leaves.

Lemon Pasta

YIELD
4 servings

TOTAL TIME
15 minutes

A few years ago, we were in Florida visiting Ryan's parents on his birthday. I asked him what he wanted for dinner and he said, "lemon pasta." I had never made him lemon pasta before, so I wasn't quite sure where that came from, but it was his birthday, so I got to working on it. All of us fell in love with this recipe, and it's become a part of our regular rotation. This is great on its own, or try it as an accompaniment to Skillet Broiled Shrimp (page 103).

Kosher salt

1 pound (455 g) spaghetti

4 tablespoons (115 g) unsalted butter

4 lemons, zested and 2 juiced

¼ cup (60 ml) half-and-half or heavy cream

½ cup (50 g) grated Parmesan cheese, plus more for serving

Freshly ground black pepper

Bring a large pot of aggressively salted water to a boil over high heat. Add the spaghetti and cook for 1 to 2 minutes less than the package instructions, until al dente. Drain and reserve ¾ cup (180 ml) of the pasta water.

While the pasta cooks, make the sauce: In a large skillet over medium heat, melt the butter. Add the lemon zest and juice. Add ½ cup (120 ml) of the pasta water and bring to a low simmer. Season with salt and pepper.

Add the pasta to the skillet and toss to coat in the sauce. Stir in the cream and the remaining ¼ cup (60 ml) pasta water if it is dry. Remove from the heat and stir in the cheese. Serve with freshly ground black pepper and more Parmesan.

Caramelized Onion Burgers

French onion soup, meet a hamburger. If you think about it, the flavors of each really compliment one another. The soup is usually made with a beef broth, and I've found that adding balsamic vinegar to the caramelized onions provides just enough of an acidic element to really balance out the fat of the beef and that glorious, ooey-gooey melted Gruyère cheese.

YIELD
4 servings

ACTIVE TIME
35 minutes

TOTAL TIME
50 to 60 minutes

For the onions:

1 tablespoon extra-virgin olive oil

1 Vidalia onion, thinly sliced

¼ cup (60 ml) beef broth

3 tablespoons sugar

1 tablespoon balsamic vinegar

Kosher salt and freshly ground black pepper

For the burgers:

1½ pounds (680 g) ground chuck

2 tablespoons grated onion

1 tablespoon dry French onion soup mix

1 cup (110 g) shredded Gruyère cheese

4 potato hamburger buns, toasted

1 cup (20 g) loosely packed arugula

Make the onions: Heat the oil in a large skillet over medium-high heat. Add the onion and sauté until it begins to brown, 4 to 5 minutes. Add the broth and use a wooden spoon to release any browned bits from the bottom of the skillet. Stir in the sugar and reduce the heat to low. Cook, stirring occasionally, until the onions are caramelized, about 20 minutes. Stir in the vinegar and season to taste with salt and pepper. Remove from the heat.

Make the burgers: Put the beef, onion, and soup mix in a bowl and mix to combine. Shape into 4 equal patties.

Preheat a griddle or cast iron skillet over medium-high heat. Add the burgers and cook for 5 to 7 minutes, until browned, then flip, top with the cheese, and cover the burgers (if on a griddle, I use a metal mixing bowl to dome over the burgers). Cook until the cheese is melted and the burgers are the desired doneness, 4 to 6 minutes more. Serve on the buns with the caramelized onions and arugula.

Surf-and-Turf Skewers with Spicy Bourbon BBQ Sauce

YIELD
8 skewers

ACTIVE TIME
25 minutes

TOTAL TIME
25 minutes

These surf-and-turf skewers are spicy, tangy, and sweet. They are perfect for a festive summer barbecue when you want an alternative to the usual. It's important when doing any kind of kebab that all of the ingredients cook at a similar rate, and the beef and shrimp are a great pairing. If you like your beef more on the done side, just do skewers of all meat and skewers of all shrimp. The grilled oranges really add a nice touch.

For the bourbon BBQ sauce:

¾ cup (180 ml) BBQ sauce

¼ cup (60 ml) bourbon

2 tablespoons fresh orange juice

2 tablespoons honey

2 teaspoons Dijon mustard

2 teaspoons sriracha

2 cloves garlic, grated

For the skewers:

32 extra-large shrimp (about 1½ pounds/680 g), peeled and deveined, tail on

2 strip steaks (about 1½ pounds/680 g), cut into 1-inch (2.5 cm) cubes to make 32 pieces

Kosher salt and freshly ground black pepper

Canola oil, for brushing the grill grates

1 navel orange, cut into wedges

3 scallions, sliced

Special equipment: Gas grill and eight 10- to 12-inch (25 to 30.5 cm) metal skewers (or bamboo skewers that have been soaked in water)

Preheat a gas grill to high.

Make the bourbon BBQ sauce: Put all the ingredients in a medium bowl and whisk to combine. Reserve ¼ cup (60 ml) of the sauce to drizzle on the finished skewers.

Make the skewers: Skewer alternating pieces of shrimp and steak on each skewer until you have 4 pieces of each per skewer. Put the skewers on a baking sheet or in a 9 by 13-inch (23 by 33 cm) baking dish. Lightly season with salt and season generously with pepper. Brush the skewers with some of the remaining sauce.

Brush the grill grates with oil. Grill the orange wedges until grill-marked and slightly charred, 2 to 3 minutes per side; set aside. Grill the shrimp and steak skewers for about 2 minutes. Flip and brush with more of the remaining sauce and grill for another 2 minutes. Turn the heat to medium-low and grill the skewers an additional 1 to 2 minutes per side, basting with more sauce.

Transfer the skewers to a platter and garnish with the oranges and scallions. Drizzle with the reserved BBQ sauce.

Grilled Farmers' Market "Paella"

YIELD
4 to 6 servings

ACTIVE TIME
30 minutes

TOTAL TIME
45 minutes

This is one of my all-time favorite summer meals. The colors are bright, and the dish feels very of the season and festive. If you have a paella pan, use it; otherwise, a big cast-iron skillet works great. Put it in the center of your table and pour a few glasses of white wine. Dinner is served! (P.S. If you can find lemon basil, it makes the dish extra special, but regular basil is perfectly A-okay!)

4 whole chicken leg quarters (drumsticks with thighs connected)

2 links sweet Italian sausage

2 links hot Italian sausage

4 tablespoons (60 ml) canola oil

Kosher salt and freshly ground black pepper

4 cups (630 g) cooked rice (leftover rice works great)

6 slices cooked bacon, chopped

2 ears corn, kernels cut from the cobs

1 bunch scallions, white and light green parts, thinly sliced

1 zucchini, sliced ½ inch (12 mm) thick diagonally

1 yellow squash, sliced ½ inch (12 mm) thick diagonally

1 pint (290 g) cherry tomatoes (yellow or red)

6 sun-dried tomatoes, chopped

1 cup (50 g) minced fresh herbs (I like lemon basil, flat-leaf parsley, and cilantro)

Zest and juice of 1 lemon

Preheat a grill to medium-high. Drizzle the chicken legs and sausage links with 1 tablespoon of the oil. Season the chicken with salt and pepper. Grill the chicken and sausage until cooked through, 20 to 25 minutes. Remove to a sheet pan to rest for 5 minutes, then slice the sausage ½ inch (12 mm) thick.

In a large bowl, combine the rice, bacon, corn, and scallions. Coat a 12-inch (30.5 cm) cast-iron skillet with 1 tablespoon oil. Add the rice mixture to the skillet and press it evenly onto the bottom of the skillet using a measuring cup. Place the skillet onto the hot grill; do not stir. Let the skillet sit on the heat until a dark brown, crispy crust forms underneath the rice, about 25 minutes.

Toss the zucchini and squash with 1 tablespoon oil and season with salt and pepper. Do the same with the cherry tomatoes. Grill the zucchini and squash until tender, 4 to 5 minutes per side. Grill the cherry tomatoes until beginning to char slightly, about 4 minutes. Remove to the sheet pan with the chicken and sausage.

Scatter the sun-dried tomatoes and fresh herbs over the rice and sprinkle with the lemon zest and juice. Place the chicken, sausage, tomatoes, zucchini, and squash on the rice. Use a spatula to scrape the bottom of the rice from the skillet and toss the mixture before serving.

Simple Mashed
Potatoes

142

Cornbread Dressing
with Herb Butter

143

Kale Slaw

145

Fondant Potatoes

146

Roasted Brussels
Sprouts with Fresno
Chile, Capers, and
Parmesan

149

Mushroom and Pea
Cauliflower "Risotto"

150

Soy and Lemon
Roasted Broccoli

152

Peach, Bourbon,
and Bacon
Baked Beans

153

Sweet Potatoes
with Cumin Yogurt,
Pomegranates, and
Pistachios

154

Herbed
Oven Fries

156

Creamed Spinach

157

Crunchy Ranch
Corn on the Cob

158

Grilled Eggplant
with Lemon,
Tahini, and Mint

160

Roasted Red Curry
Acorn Squash

161

Broccoli
au Gratin

162

Miso Twice-Baked
Japanese
Sweet Potatoes

164

Swiss Chard
with Almonds
and Raisins

165

chapter four

———

SIDES

Simple Mashed Potatoes

YIELD
4 to 6 servings

TOTAL TIME
40 minutes

My grandma and her sister, my great-aunt Pat, make the best mashed potatoes on the planet. Whenever we had a family dinner, there would be a pot of a minimum of ten pounds of mashed potatoes, and no matter how much was made, there would be none left at the end of the meal. Sadly, my grandma suffers from Alzheimer's, so I am no longer able to ask her for her cooking secrets, but I was lucky enough to have learned as much as I could from her in the past. I had never quite mastered mashed potatoes, though, so I called on Pat and asked her for the secret. I presumed it would be heavy cream and a massive amount of butter, but I was wrong. Pat said she uses hot 2% milk rather than cream. She said the lower fat content actually makes for lighter, fluffier mashed potatoes. There is plenty of butter for flavor. She uses an electric mixer to whip the potatoes; just be sure to stop as soon as they reach a creamy texture, because it is easy to go into gummy territory if you whip for too long.

4 russet potatoes, peeled and cut into 1-inch (2.5 cm) chunks

2 tablespoons kosher salt, plus more to taste

1 cup (240 ml) hot 2% milk

½ cup (1 stick/115 g) unsalted butter, at room temperature, cut into pieces

Put the potatoes and 2 tablespoons of the salt in a large saucepan and cover with cold water, 1 inch (2.5 cm) over the top of the potatoes. Bring to a boil over medium-high heat, then reduce the heat and simmer for 25 to 30 minutes, until fork tender (it is important not to undercook the potatoes). Drain the potatoes, then transfer them to a large mixing bowl. Pour the hot milk over the potatoes and whip with an electric mixer for 2½ minutes, adding the butter a few pieces at a time and scraping down the sides when needed. Season with additional salt if desired (about 1 teaspoon), and serve.

Cornbread Dressing with Herb Butter

YIELD
8 servings

ACTIVE TIME
35 minutes

TOTAL TIME
1 hour 15 minutes

Do you say "stuffing" or "dressing"? I say stuffing for inside the bird, dressing for baked separately. I like to put a handful inside the bird just for flavoring, then bake the rest in a pan so that it gets all those nice crispy bits. Whatever your choice is, this cornbread stuffing/dressing will not disappoint. In the past when we haven't hosted the holiday at our house, I've either asked to be in charge of the dressing, or made it anyway just to have at home as our own "leftovers." I learned from my great-grandmother Pearl that the most important flavoring for dressing is sage. You can make your own homemade cornbread, but this is a good time to cut a corner and use a mix or store-bought. If you have a Whole Foods near you, I've found that the cornbread in their deli section is delicious and perfect for this recipe.

¼ cup (55 g) Herb Butter (recipe follows)

2 yellow onions, finely diced

2 ribs celery, finely diced

6 cups (210 g) cubed cornbread (store-bought or homemade)

¾ cup (180 ml) low-sodium chicken broth

½ cup (120 ml) whole milk

1 large egg, lightly beaten

½ teaspoon kosher salt

½ teaspoon freshly ground black pepper

Melt the herb butter in a medium skillet over medium heat. Add the onions and celery and sauté until translucent, stirring occasionally, 10 to 15 minutes. Remove from the heat and let cool.

In a large bowl, combine the onions and celery with the cornbread, broth, milk, egg, salt, and pepper. Mix well to combine. Refrigerate until ready to bake.

Preheat the oven to 375°F (190°C). Grease a 9 by 13-inch (23 by 33 cm) baking dish.

Transfer the stuffing mixture to the prepared baking dish. Bake until golden brown, 35 to 40 minutes, and serve warm.

Herb Butter

YIELD: ABOUT 1 CUP (250 G)

Save any leftover herb butter to rub on roast chicken or spread on a baguette or toast.

1 cup (2 sticks/225 g) unsalted butter, softened

3 tablespoons minced fresh sage

2 tablespoons minced fresh flat-leaf parsley

2 tablespoons minced fresh thyme

1 teaspoon minced fresh rosemary

2 tablespoons kosher salt

2 teaspoons freshly ground black pepper

Combine all the ingredients in a small mixing bowl. Mix to blend. Cover and refrigerate until ready to serve.

Kale Slaw

YIELD
4 servings

TOTAL TIME
15 minutes

By now you probably know my affection for kale. I really can't get enough of it. This coleslaw started as a kale salad when I was cooking for a group and wanted to make a salad but didn't have enough kale. I cut it with a head of cabbage and then got the idea to do coleslaw. Using half mayonnaise and half Greek yogurt helps to lighten it up a bit while still giving it that wonderfully rich mayonnaise taste.

½ cup (120 ml) mayonnaise

½ cup (120 ml) Greek yogurt

2 tablespoons Dijon mustard

2 tablespoons apple cider vinegar

1 teaspoon honey

½ teaspoon celery seeds

½ teaspoon kosher salt

¼ teaspoon freshly ground black pepper

5 cups (335 g) shredded kale

3 cups (280 g) shredded cabbage

3 cups (335 g) shredded carrots

½ cup (70 g) sunflower seeds

Combine the mayonnaise, yogurt, mustard, vinegar, honey, celery seeds, salt, and pepper in a bowl. Mix to blend. Put the kale, cabbage, carrots, and sunflower seeds in a large bowl and pour in the dressing. Toss to combine until everything is evenly coated, then serve or store in the fridge for 2 to 3 days.

Fondant Potatoes

YIELD
4 servings

ACTIVE TIME
10 minutes

TOTAL TIME
40 minutes

These are fancy potatoes. They sound fancy, they look fancy, and they taste fancy. But in this instance, fancy doesn't mean intricate or complicated. You know when you go to a French restaurant and the potatoes are always just perfect—perfectly browned and crispy on the outside and perfectly soft and luscious on the inside—but at home you can never quite get them the same? Well, I've cracked the code. They're seared in a hot skillet, then braised in broth and (you guessed it) butter. Enjoy the oohs and ahhs of your guests!

4 russet potatoes

Kosher salt and cracked black pepper

2 tablespoons vegetable oil

10 tablespoons (140 g) unsalted butter

1 cup (240 ml) low-sodium chicken broth

2 sprigs fresh rosemary

2 cloves garlic, whole

Flaky sea salt

Preheat the oven to 400°F (205°C).

Peel the potatoes and slice off the ends. Cut into 1-inch (2.5 cm) slices. Season both sides of the potatoes generously with kosher salt and pepper.

Heat a cast-iron skillet (or other heavy-duty, ovenproof skillet) over medium-high heat. Add the oil and 4 tablespoons (55 g) of the butter. Sear the potatoes on one side until golden brown, about 4 minutes. Flip the potatoes and add the broth, rosemary, and garlic. Cut the remaining 6 tablespoons (85 g) butter into cubes and scatter on top of the potatoes. Transfer the skillet to the oven and cook until fork-tender, about 30 minutes. Transfer to a serving platter, spoon the pan sauce all over the potatoes, garnish with flaky salt, and serve hot.

Roasted Brussels Sprouts with Fresno Chile, Capers, and Parmesan

YIELD
4 servings

TOTAL TIME
35 minutes

I'm so glad Brussels sprouts had a renaissance a few years ago. They were one of those vegetables that just seemed doomed to a legacy of steamed, overcooked, mush but were saved by roasting! I really like adding a kick with Fresno chiles and some brininess from capers—and a little Parmesan umami never hurt anything. This recipe works great with broccoli as well (another vegetable that easily could have suffered the same fate).

1½ pounds (680 g) Brussels sprouts, halved

1 Fresno chile, thinly sliced

1 tablespoon capers, drained, rinsed, and chopped

2 tablespoons extra-virgin olive oil

¾ teaspoon kosher salt

⅛ teaspoon cracked black pepper

¼ cup (25 g) grated Parmesan cheese

Preheat the oven to 425°F (220°C). Line a baking sheet with parchment paper.

Toss the Brussels sprouts with the chile, capers, oil, salt, and pepper in a large bowl. Transfer to the prepared baking sheet. Bake for 15 minutes, then stir and flip. Sprinkle the cheese over the vegetables and toss to coat. Bake for another 10 to 12 minutes, until the Brussels sprouts are browned and the cheese is crisp and golden. Serve immediately.

Mushroom and Pea Cauliflower "Risotto"

When the cauliflower risotto trend started, I was first in line to buy a ticket and hop on the train. I keep bags of cauliflower rice in my freezer, and whenever I need a quick side dish, especially on a weeknight, I sauté it in a skillet with a little butter. For something a little more special, I like to cook it in the style of "risotto," like this. It gets creamy and, while not exactly like the real thing, it certainly does the trick.

YIELD
4 servings

ACTIVE TIME
30 minutes

TOTAL TIME
30 minutes

1 head cauliflower, stem removed

3 tablespoons unsalted butter

1 clove garlic, smashed but left whole

8 ounces (225 g) sliced mushrooms

Kosher salt and freshly ground black pepper

½ cup (75 g) shelled green peas

1 cup (240 ml) low-sodium chicken or vegetable broth

½ cup (50 g) grated Parmesan cheese

Cut the cauliflower into chunks. Working in batches, pulse the cauliflower in a food processor until coarse in texture, like rice. Reserve 4 cups (200 g) for this recipe and save any leftovers for another use.

In a large skillet over medium heat, melt 2 tablespoons of the butter with the garlic. Stir in the mushrooms and cook until browned, 5 to 7 minutes. Remove and discard the garlic, then season the mushrooms with salt and pepper.

Increase the heat to medium-high and stir in the cauliflower. Sauté for 1 to 2 minutes. Add ½ cup (120 ml) of the broth and simmer until the liquid has mostly evaporated, 8 to 10 minutes. Stir in the peas and the remaining ½ cup (120 ml) broth. Simmer until the liquid is almost gone. Remove from the heat, season with salt and pepper, and stir in the remaining 1 tablespoon butter and half of the cheese, stirring until the cheese has melted. Stir in the remaining cheese. Serve hot.

Soy and Lemon Roasted Broccoli

YIELD
4 servings

ACTIVE TIME
5 minutes

TOTAL TIME
35 minutes

My mom was the queen of burning broccoli. I always knew when she was making it for dinner because suddenly the house would be filled with the scent of sulphur. Every time, she'd yell out, "Oh no, the broccoli is burning!" But did she ever learn? No. She cooked it in a covered saucepan with just an inch or so of water, trying her best to steam it. Little did we know, she was ahead of the curve. Now we love burnt broccoli! (Just not in a saucepan; roasted in the oven is much better.) The addition of soy sauce gives the broccoli a little umami, and lemon juice adds a bright flavor. If you have amino acids in your fridge (like Bragg's), I like to use that in place of the soy sometimes as well.

2 tablespoons olive oil

2 tablespoons fresh lemon juice

2 tablespoons soy sauce

1 head broccoli, separated into florets (save the stems for broccoli "rice"; see Note)

Preheat the oven to 425°F (220°C). Line a baking sheet with parchment paper.

In a medium bowl, whisk the oil, lemon juice, and soy sauce. Add the broccoli and toss to coat. Transfer to the prepared baking sheet. Bake for 30 minutes, stirring once halfway through. Serve hot.

Note: To make broccoli "rice," cut the stalks into 1-inch (2.5 cm) pieces and put in a food processor. Pulse until the broccoli is the consistency of rice. Sauté in a skillet with a little olive oil and desired flavoring.

Peach, Bourbon, and Bacon Baked Beans

YIELD
6 servings

ACTIVE TIME
20 minutes

TOTAL TIME
1 hour 5 minutes

Get ready, because these beans are about to be your new favorite. They are everything you ever wanted baked beans to be but they never were, with just the right balance of sweet to tangy, a touch of fruit, and smoke from the bacon. Take these to your next potluck or add them to your Fourth of July buffet and you will be the hero of the party.

3 slices bacon, diced

1 onion, chopped

Three 15-ounce (425 g) cans great northern beans, drained and rinsed

1 cup (240 ml) ketchup

1 cup (220 g) packed dark brown sugar

1 cup (240 ml) peach preserves

¾ cup (180 ml) chicken broth

¼ cup (60 ml) bourbon

2 teaspoons dry mustard

1½ teaspoons kosher salt

½ teaspoon freshly ground black pepper

¼ teaspoon garlic powder

Preheat the oven to 350°F (175°C).

In a Dutch oven, cook the bacon over medium heat until the fat is rendered, 8 to 10 minutes. Transfer the bacon to a paper towel–lined plate and set aside. Add the onion to the pot and cook until translucent, about 10 minutes.

Reduce the heat to low, add the beans, ketchup, brown sugar, preserves, broth, bourbon, mustard, salt, pepper, garlic powder, and bacon and stir until well combined. Bring to a simmer. Cover and bake for 40 minutes. Stir before serving.

Sweet Potatoes with Cumin Yogurt, Pomegranates, and Pistachios

We eat quite a few sweet potatoes in this household. I find they make an easy side just cut into wedges, tossed with some seasoning, and roasted. In fact, you can stop right there in this recipe. When I'm feeling a little extra, I give them the special treatment and dress them up a bit. The smokiness of the cumin is a great combination with the spice of the chili powder and the sweetness of the potatoes, cooled off by the creamy yogurt, and then a little "pop" from the pomegranates. Sprinkle with pistachios for some nuttiness, because why not? Treat yourself!

YIELD
4 to 6 servings

ACTIVE TIME
10 minutes

TOTAL TIME
40 minutes

3 sweet potatoes, cut into quarters

2 tablespoons olive oil

½ teaspoon chili powder

½ teaspoon kosher salt

¼ teaspoon freshly ground black pepper

½ cup (120 ml) Greek yogurt

¼ teaspoon ground cumin

1 clove garlic, grated

1 tablespoon fresh lemon juice

1 teaspoon honey

1 tablespoon minced fresh cilantro

¼ cup (45 g) pomegranate seeds

2 tablespoons chopped pistachios

Preheat the oven to 425°F (220°C). Line a baking sheet with parchment paper.

In a large bowl, toss the sweet potatoes with the oil, chili powder, salt, and pepper. Transfer to the prepared baking sheet. Roast until golden brown and tender, about 30 minutes.

In a small bowl, combine the yogurt, cumin, garlic, lemon juice, honey, and cilantro.

Serve the sweet potatoes on a platter, dolloped with the cumin yogurt and garnished with pomegranate seeds and pistachios.

Herbed Oven Fries

YIELD

4 servings

TOTAL TIME

30 minutes

Praise the Lord for French fries. They are truly my weakness. I want them to be really salty and served with tons of ketchup. Maybe ketchup is actually my weakness, and the fries are just a vehicle. I digress. When I've tried making fries in the oven in the past, they've been good but not great. Now I think I've cracked the code with this recipe. I was too stingy with the oil in the past. I thought if I was making them in the oven, that meant I should only be using a drizzle. Those potatoes really need more like ¼ cup (60 ml) of oil. It's still way less than frying, so just go for it. The garlic salt and parsley make them taste restaurant quality. Enjoy!

2 russet potatoes, cut into sticks ½ inch (12 mm) thick

¼ cup (60 ml) olive oil

1 teaspoon garlic salt

1 tablespoon chopped fresh parsley

Ketchup, for serving

Preheat the oven to 425°F (220°C). Put a rimmed baking sheet in the oven and let it heat while the oven heats.

Toss the potato slices with the oil and garlic salt. Remove the heated pan from the oven and spread the potatoes out on the pan in an even layer. Bake for 15 minutes, then flip the potatoes and bake for another 15 minutes, or until both sides are toasted and brown. Transfer the potatoes to a large bowl and toss with the parsley. Serve with plenty of ketchup!

Creamed Spinach

YIELD
4 servings

TOTAL TIME
10 minutes

I'm a big fan of a steakhouse meal. Not because I look forward to a giant piece of sizzling steak, but because I love the sides: a big loaded baked potato, maybe some sautéed mushrooms, and always an order of creamed spinach. I usually take home my leftover spinach and put it in an omelet the next day for breakfast. When making it at home, I use frozen spinach instead of fresh, since it is already cooked down.

2 tablespoons unsalted butter

1 shallot, minced

2 cloves garlic, minced

1 pound (455 g) frozen spinach, thawed

1 teaspoon kosher salt, or more to taste

¼ teaspoon cracked black pepper, or more to taste

1½ cups (360 ml) heavy cream

¼ teaspoon grated nutmeg

Melt the butter in a large skillet over medium heat. Add the shallot and cook until softened, about 2 minutes, then add the garlic and cook for 1 minute. Stir in the spinach and cook until warm, 3 to 4 minutes, stirring occasionally. Add the salt and pepper and stir. Pour in the cream and sprinkle in the nutmeg. Cook until the cream is thickened and simmering, about 3 minutes. Season with additional salt and pepper, if desired. Serve immediately.

Crunchy Ranch Corn on the Cob

YIELD
4 servings

TOTAL TIME
5 minutes

When I was a kid, my number-one snack was Cool Ranch Doritos. My mom would never buy them for me, but when I spent the weekend at my dad's house, he always got them for me. I was perfectly fine playing my divorced parents off of each other if it meant that I got to have my Doritos. Instead of taking my time over the weekend to really enjoy the bag, I usually gorged myself as soon as we got home from the store. I do remember one occasion when I ate the entire bag in one sitting. Now that I'm an adult, I'm only slightly better at controlling myself around the power of the Cool Ranch, but I've found that they make a wicked coating for everything from a chicken breast to a piece of corn on the cob. This is a great way to use up the crumbs at the bottom of the bag.

4 ears corn, cooked (grilled or boiled)

¼ cup (60 ml) Ranch Dressing (homemade, page 49, or store-bought)

1 cup (35 g) crushed ranch-flavored corn chips

Brush each ear of corn with about 1 tablespoon of the dressing.

Spread the crushed chips on a plate and roll each ear of corn in the chips to completely coat each ear. Serve.

Grilled Eggplant with Lemon, Tahini, and Mint

YIELD
4 servings

ACTIVE TIME
10 minutes

TOTAL TIME
25 minutes

This recipe does double duty: If you have a vegetarian friend coming for dinner, you can make this and serve it both as a side dish and as a main dish. It goes great with grilled chicken (use the same spiced oil mixture on the chicken, just double the recipe for it), and an eggplant half is hearty enough to serve as an entrée with a couple of sides. If pomegranate seeds are in season, I like to throw those on for garnish.

2 eggplants, stem on, cut in half lengthwise

2 tablespoons extra-virgin olive oil, plus more for drizzling

1 lemon, zested and cut into quarters

½ teaspoon smoked paprika

¼ teaspoon ground cumin

½ teaspoon kosher salt

Freshly ground black pepper

2 tablespoons tahini

Flaky sea salt

¼ cup (13 g) fresh mint leaves

Preheat a grill for direct (medium-high) and indirect (medium-low) cooking. Use a knife to make crosshatch marks on the flesh side of each eggplant half. In a small bowl, mix the oil, lemon zest, paprika, cumin, kosher salt, and pepper. Use a pastry brush to coat both sides of the eggplant and the lemon wedges with the oil mixture.

Place the eggplant, flesh side down, on direct heat on the grill for 5 minutes. Flip and cook for 5 minutes more, then move to indirect heat to cook until tender, an additional 5 minutes. Add the lemon wedges to the grill over direct heat and cook until slightly charred on each side, 2 to 3 minutes per side.

Remove the eggplant and lemon wedges to a serving plate. Drizzle with the tahini and additional oil, season with flaky salt, and garnish with mint leaves.

Roasted Red Curry Acorn Squash

YIELD

4 to 6 servings

TOTAL TIME

25 minutes

Roasted acorn squash is one of my go-to dishes in the fall. I slice up the squash, toss it with whatever kind of seasoning I'm feeling and some oil, then roast it until it's caramelized and crispy. Its sweetness goes so well with the spicy red curry paste.

1 tablespoon red curry paste

2 tablespoons extra-virgin olive oil

½ teaspoon kosher salt

2 acorn squash, cut into ½-inch (12 mm) slices

Preheat the oven to 425°F (220°C). Line two rimmed baking sheets with parchment paper.

Whisk the curry paste, oil, and salt in a large bowl. Add the squash and toss to coat. Divide between the two prepared baking sheets. Bake for 25 to 30 minutes, rotating halfway through, or until the squash is tender and browned on the edges. Remove to a plate and serve immediately.

Broccoli au Gratin

YIELD
4 to 6 servings

TOTAL TIME
45 minutes

Growing up, whenever we had a family reunion, it was what we called a "covered dish" party, which is essentially a potluck. Each person was to bring a covered dish, and there was always a huge buffet that included chicken and dumplings, mashed potatoes, and roast beef, and someone would always bring a broccoli casserole. I looooved broccoli casserole. It would have broccoli, rice, a sauce made of some sort of condensed cream soup, and would be topped with crushed Ritz crackers and shredded cheese. I decided to revive this dish and give it a little makeover by losing the canned soup and making a simple cream sauce. It takes me back!

4 heads broccoli, cut into florets

2 tablespoons extra-virgin olive oil

8 ounces (225 g) sliced mushrooms

2 teaspoons kosher salt

1 teaspoon cracked black pepper

1 teaspoon onion powder

¼ cup (55 g) unsalted butter, plus more for buttering the dish

¼ cup (30 g) all-purpose flour

2 cups (480 ml) milk

1 cup (288 g) crushed butter crackers

1 cup (115 g) shredded sharp cheddar cheese

Preheat the oven to 400°F (205°C). Butter an 8-inch (20 cm) baking dish or a gratin dish.

Bring 1 inch (2.5 cm) of water to a boil over medium high heat in a large saucepan with a steamer basket and a lid. Add the broccoli to the steamer basket, cover, and steam for 4 to 6 minutes, or until the broccoli is bright green and tender, but still crisp. Remove the broccoli to a plate and set aside.

Heat the oil in a large saucepan or skillet over medium-high heat. Add the mushrooms and cook until they have released their moisture and have started to brown, 4 to 5 minutes. Add the salt, pepper, onion powder, and butter and stir until the butter is melted. Sprinkle the flour over the mixture and stir until a paste forms. Cook for 2 to 3 more minutes, until the paste is golden brown and has a nutty aroma. Slowly pour the milk into the mixture a little at a time, stirring as you pour. Once the milk is all combined, bring to a simmer and cook for another 3 to 4 minutes, until the mixture thickens. Remove from the heat and add the broccoli, tossing to coat. Transfer the mixture to the baking dish.

Put the butter crackers and cheese in a food processor and grind into a fine crumb mixture. Sprinkle the crumbs over the top of the broccoli mixture and bake for 20 to 25 minutes, until the broccoli mixture is bubbling and the topping is browned and melty. Let cool for a few minutes before serving.

Miso Twice-Baked Japanese Sweet Potatoes

Miso paste is one of those things I keep in my fridge and use as a secret weapon. Whenever I want to add a bang of flavor, especially if I'm cooking a quick dinner, I add it in. I even put it in my chocolate chip cookies! It adds a rich depth that's salty and umami and is awesome with sweet potatoes. If your grocery store has Japanese sweet potatoes, definitely give them a try. They are a bit nutty, almost like roasted chestnuts. Any sweet potato variety will work with this recipe, though, so have fun experimenting.

YIELD
4 servings

ACTIVE TIME
10 minutes

TOTAL TIME
60 minutes

4 Japanese sweet potatoes (or any variety of sweet potato)

2 tablespoons white miso paste

2 tablespoons unsalted butter, at room temperature

2 tablespoons maple syrup

Preheat the oven to 450°F (230°C). Line a baking sheet with parchment paper.

Prick the sweet potatoes a few times with a fork. Bake on the prepared baking sheet for 45 to 50 minutes, until very tender. Turn the oven to broil.

Let cool slightly, then cut the tops off of the sweet potatoes and scoop the flesh into a bowl, leaving about ¼ inch (6 mm) of flesh on the peel. To the sweet potato in the bowl, add the miso paste, butter, and maple syrup and mix with an electric mixer, or by hand, vigorously. Spoon the mixture back into the skins. Broil the sweet potatoes for 3 to 4 minutes, until browned and bubbling. Serve warm.

Swiss Chard with Almonds and Raisins

Usually with greens, the stems are removed and discarded, but Swiss chard stems are tender enough to eat along with the leafy parts. I chop them up and give them a sauté before adding in the leaves. I like the contrast of textures, and I'm always a fan of no waste. I make this dish quite often, since it's such a healthy, quick side. You can use dried cranberries in place of the raisins, if you prefer.

YIELD
4 to 6 servings

TOTAL TIME
10 minutes

1 bunch rainbow chard

¼ cup (25 g) sliced almonds

1 tablespoon extra-virgin olive oil

1 clove garlic, minced

¼ cup (35 g) raisins

Kosher salt and cracked black pepper

Pinch of crushed red pepper

2 tablespoons red wine vinegar

Remove the leaves from the stems of the chard. Roughly chop the leaves and mince the stems.

Heat a large skillet over medium-high heat, add the almonds, and toast until browned and crisp. Remove the almonds to a bowl and set aside.

Add the oil to the skillet, heat, then add the chard stems. Sauté for 2 to 3 minutes, or until crisp tender. Add the garlic and raisins and cook for about 30 seconds. Stir in the leaves. Season with a heavy pinch of salt, the black pepper, and crushed red pepper. Add the vinegar. Cook until the leaves are wilted, and add 1 to 2 tablespoons of water to help steam the leaves. Remove from the heat and stir in the almonds. Serve warm.

Iron Skillet
Lemon Poppyseed
Soufflé

168

Pumpkin
Cheesecake

170

Chocolate Cherry
Ice Cream
Bonbons

171

No-Bake Peanut
Butter Cheesecake

172

Chocolate Croissant
Bread Pudding

175

Mocha Swirl
Ice Cream

176

Strawberry
Ice Cream

177

Grandma's
Whoopie Pies

179

Miso Chocolate
Chunk Cookies

180

Mango
Dump Cake

182

Cannoli
Trifle

183

Apple
Cobbler

185

Affogato

186

Chocolate
Pudding

189

Stone Fruit
Crisp

190

chapter five

———

DESSERTS

Iron Skillet Lemon Poppyseed Soufflé

YIELD
6 to 8 servings

TOTAL TIME
45 minutes

Tucked away in the Brentwood Country Mart in Los Angeles is a restaurant and market called Farmshop. It is everything I love about California cuisine: loads of inventive, fresh vegetable dishes and creative takes on classics. For dessert, I always order their Viennese-style soufflé pancake. It comes in a beautiful iron skillet with fresh berries and cream. It is simply divine. I tried (and tried . . . and tried . . .) to re-create it at home, and I think I've gotten pretty close. I added lemon and poppyseed to my version.

4 large eggs, separated

⅛ teaspoon cream of tartar

½ cup (65 g) confectioners' sugar, plus more for serving

¾ cup (150 g) granulated sugar

Zest of 2 lemons

1 tablespoon poppyseeds

1 teaspoon vanilla extract

1½ cups (360 ml) heavy cream

¼ cup (30 g) cornstarch

1 cup (125 g) self-rising flour

¼ teaspoon kosher salt

4 tablespoons (55 g) unsalted butter

Fresh berries and whipped cream, for serving

Preheat the oven to 350°F (175°C).

Beat the egg whites with the cream of tartar and confectioners' sugar in a stand mixer (or in a bowl with an electric hand mixer) until stiff peaks form. In a separate bowl, whisk the egg yolks, granulated sugar, lemon zest, poppyseeds, vanilla, cream, cornstarch, flour, and salt together until smooth. Fold the egg whites into the yolk mixture until combined.

Melt the butter in a 12-inch (30.5 cm) cast-iron skillet over medium heat. Swirl the butter around the skillet until it is completely coated. Add the batter and cook until the bottom starts to set up and the edges brown and come away from the sides, 3 to 4 minutes. Run a spatula around the edges to separate it from the sides. Transfer to the oven and bake for 25 to 30 minutes—don't open the oven! The soufflé will puff slightly and will be set in the center and golden on top. Let cool slightly, then sprinkle with confectioners' sugar. Slice and serve with more confectioners' sugar, fresh berries, and whipped cream.

Pumpkin Cheesecake

YIELD
8 servings

ACTIVE TIME
10 minutes

TOTAL TIME
4 hours and
50 minutes,
up to overnight

This recipe is inspired by my mom's Lemony Berry Cheesecake that was in my *Endless Summer Cookbook*. It is made in the blender, so it's pretty much the easiest cheesecake ever. Her recipe is a bit more virtuous (she doesn't add butter to the crust, she uses light cottage cheese and cream cheese, which you could totally use here too, and she uses less sugar). This is the perfect Thanksgiving dessert when you want something a little different than the usual pumpkin pie.

1 cup (90 g) crushed gingersnap cookies

2 tablespoons unsalted butter, melted

2 cups (480 ml) cottage cheese

One 8-ounce (226 g) package cream cheese

3 large eggs

1 cup (200 g) sugar

1 cup (245 g) pure pumpkin puree

2 teaspoons pumpkin pie spice

2 tablespoons all-purpose flour

1 teaspoon vanilla extract

Whipped cream, for serving

Preheat the oven to 375°F (190°C). Spray a 9-inch (23 cm) springform pan with cooking spray.

In a small bowl, mix the cookies with the butter and transfer to the prepared pan. Use a measuring cup to gently press the crumbs into an even layer.

In a blender, combine the cottage cheese, cream cheese, eggs, sugar, pumpkin puree, pumpkin pie spice, flour, and vanilla. Pour into the crust and bake for 40 minutes. Let cool completely. Chill in the refrigerator for at least 4 hours or up to overnight.

Serve the cheesecake with a dollop of whipped cream.

Chocolate Cherry Ice Cream Bonbons

YIELD
24 servings

ACTIVE TIME
40 minutes

TOTAL TIME
3 hours 40 minutes
(includes freezing time)

I want a day to just sit around and eat bonbons. I've always heard that expression but never actually known anyone to do it. Can't I be the one? These would be my bonbons of choice. You can easily swap flavors in this recipe; try it with cookies and cream or cookie dough ice cream as well.

24 chocolate wafer cookies

1 quart (960 ml) chocolate cherry ice cream, softened

Chocolate shell ice cream sauce (recipe follows)

Special equipment: one 24-count or two 12-count mini muffin pans

Spray a 24-count mini muffin pan with nonstick cooking spray. Place a 20-inch-long (50 cm) piece of plastic wrap over the muffin pan, leaving about 4 inches (10 cm) of excess plastic hanging over the ends of the pan. Press the plastic into each cup of the pan, making sure the cups are completely lined with the plastic wrap.

Using a small ice cream scoop or tablespoon measure, scoop ice cream into each muffin cup. Use a small offset spatula or butter knife to spread the ice cream into the tin. Place a chocolate cookie on top of each ice cream–filled muffin cup. Freeze until the ice cream hardens, about 3 hours.

Place a rectangular cooling rack over a baking sheet. Line a second baking sheet with parchment paper.

Carefully remove the plastic wrap from the muffin pan to release the bonbons from the muffin cups. Place the bonbons cookie-side down on the baking sheet lined with the cooling rack. Slowly pour some of the chocolate shell ice cream sauce over about half of the bonbons to cover completely. Repeat on the second half until all 24 are coated.

Transfer the bonbons from the cooling rack to the parchment-lined baking sheet with an offset spatula or butter knife and put in the freezer until set, 3 to 5 minutes. Dip the offset spatula in hot water, then use it to remove the bonbons from the parchment. The hot spatula will help prevent the chocolate shell of the bonbons from cracking when you remove them. Store in a resealable container in the freezer until ready to serve.

Chocolate Shell Ice Cream Sauce
YIELD: ABOUT 1 CUP (235 ML)

8 ounces (225 g) semisweet chocolate, chopped

½ cup (120 ml) coconut oil

2 tablespoons corn syrup

Melt the chocolate in a double boiler. Stir in the coconut oil and corn syrup. Let cool for 1 hour. It should be the consistency of pancake batter.

No-Bake Peanut Butter Cheesecake

I judged a baking series for the Food Network in which the contestants were to exclusively use Girl Scout cookies as inspiration and as an ingredient. I took home an obscene amount of cookies. You'd think it would be an easy feat to polish them all off, but eventually I had to come up with some recipes to use them up. I used the Do-Si-Dos peanut butter sandwich cookies to make a no-bake peanut butter cheesecake, and it was *fab*. So fab that I made Ryan take it to work so that I would stop eating it. He said it was gone from the break room in mere minutes.

YIELD
8 servings

ACTIVE TIME
15 minutes

TOTAL TIME
6 hours 45 minutes
(includes freezing time)

1 cup (90 g) finely crushed peanut butter sandwich cookies (about 22 cookies), plus an additional 3 tablespoons crushed cookies for garnish

Two 8-ounce (226 g) packages cream cheese, at room temperature

1 cup (240 ml) creamy peanut butter

½ cup (65 g) confectioners' sugar

One 8-ounce (226 g) tub whipped topping

Spray a 10-inch (25 cm) springform pan with nonstick cooking spray. Spread the crushed cookies into the bottom, using a metal measuring cup to press into an even layer. Freeze for 30 minutes.

Using an electric mixer on medium-high speed, beat the cream cheese, peanut butter, and confectioners' sugar until fluffy, about 5 minutes. Using a rubber spatula, fold in the whipped topping. Transfer the mixture to the springform pan. Use a spatula to smooth into an even layer. Top with the remaining cookies. Cover with plastic wrap and refrigerate for at least 6 hours, until set. Remove from the pan, cut, and serve.

Chocolate Croissant Bread Pudding

Okay, if you don't make a single other dessert from this book, make this bread pudding. It is D E C A D E N T and F A B U L O U S. I made it one day and put it on my Instagram story and I don't think I've ever gotten so many DMs asking for a recipe (but I waited until now to share it!). This is my nod to Meryl Streep making chocolate croissants for Steve Martin in *It's Complicated*, the inspiration for this entire book.

YIELD
6 servings

ACTIVE TIME
10 minutes

TOTAL TIME
1 hour 55 minutes

3 cups (720 ml) half-and-half

6 large eggs

½ cup (100 g) sugar

1 teaspoon vanilla extract

½ teaspoon ground cinnamon

¼ teaspoon kosher salt

6 chocolate croissants, cut into 1½-inch (4 cm) pieces

1 cup (170 g) semisweet chocolate chunks

Whipped cream or vanilla ice cream, for serving (optional)

Spray an 8-inch (20 cm) square baking dish with nonstick cooking spray.

In a large bowl, whisk the half-and-half, eggs, sugar, vanilla, cinnamon, and salt. Add the croissant pieces and chocolate chunks and toss to coat. Transfer to the prepared baking dish. Press the mixture down into the pan. Cover and refrigerate for 1 hour to allow the liquid to be absorbed.

Preheat the oven to 350°F (175°C).

Bake for 40 to 45 minutes, until golden brown. Serve hot with whipped cream or vanilla ice cream, if desired.

Mocha Swirl Ice Cream

YIELD
6 to 8 servings

ACTIVE TIME
15 minutes

TOTAL TIME
6 hours 35 minutes
(includes freezing
time)

Ryan loves coffee-flavored ice cream, so I started making this for him. I was never much of a coffee ice cream eater because I was always worried that it had caffeine and I'd be up all night after I ate it; that's why I use decaf instant coffee in this recipe. All of the flavor, none of the buzz! The hot fudge makes it super decadent and it looks so pretty. I may or may not serve it with extra fudge on top.

1 pint (480 ml) heavy cream

2 tablespoons instant coffee (I use decaf)

1 teaspoon coffee extract

1 teaspoon vanilla extract

One 14-ounce (397 g) can sweetened condensed milk

½ cup (120 ml) jarred hot fudge

Line a 9 by 5-inch (23 by 12 cm) loaf pan with plastic wrap, letting the edges hang over and allowing enough extra plastic to wrap the ice cream.

Reserve 1 tablespoon of the heavy cream. In a large bowl, combine the instant coffee, coffee extract, vanilla, and the remaining cream. Use an electric mixer to whip until medium to firm peaks form. Use a spatula to gently fold in the condensed milk. Transfer half of the mixture to the prepared loaf pan and freeze until just beginning to set, about 20 minutes.

Microwave the hot fudge with the reserved 1 tablespoon heavy cream in a microwave-safe bowl for 20 to 25 seconds, just to loosen it slightly. Spoon it lengthwise down the center of the pan, from end to end.

Transfer the remaining cream mixture to the loaf pan on top of the fudge. Use a butter knife to make swirls going through the mixture. (This will move the fudge throughout the mixture.) Wrap with plastic wrap and place in the freezer for 6 hours. Scoop and serve.

Strawberry Ice Cream

YIELD
6 to 8 servings

ACTIVE TIME
10 minutes

TOTAL TIME
6 hours 10 minutes
(includes freezing
time)

1 cup (165 g) chopped fresh
strawberries, plus 1 cup
(165 g) sliced

1 teaspoon vanilla extract

1 pint (480 ml) heavy cream

One 14-ounce (397 g) can
sweetened condensed
milk

Line a 9 by 5-inch (23 by 12 cm)
loaf pan with plastic wrap, letting
the edges hang over and allowing
enough extra plastic to wrap the ice
cream.

In a large bowl, combine the cream
and vanilla. Use an electric mixer
to whip until medium to firm peaks
form. Use a spatula to gently fold
in the condensed milk and chopped
strawberries. Transfer the mixture
to the prepared loaf pan, wrap
with plastic wrap, and place in the
freezer for 6 hours.

Before serving, let stand at room
temperature for 5 minutes.
Unwrap the plastic, invert onto
a serving plate, and remove the
plastic entirely. Place the sliced
strawberries on top of the loaf and
serve immediately.

Grandma's Whoopie Pies

My grandma's whoopie pies were legendary. She didn't make them that often, but when she did, word traveled fast. She would wrap them individually in plastic wrap and when you got yours, you savored every bite of it, not only because it was so good, but because you didn't know when you'd be getting them again—and you certainly weren't going to get a second one.

YIELD
20 to 24 whoopie pies

ACTIVE TIME
45 minutes

TOTAL TIME
2 hours (includes chilling time)

For the cookies:

2 cups (255 g) all-purpose flour

½ cup (50 g) cocoa powder

1½ teaspoons baking soda

½ teaspoon baking powder

½ teaspoon kosher salt

1 cup (200 g) sugar

½ cup (1 stick/115 g) unsalted butter, at room temperature

1 large egg

1 teaspoon vanilla extract

1 cup (240 ml) milk

For the filling:

2 cups (250 g) confectioners' sugar

⅔ cup (10 2/3 tablespoons/150 g) unsalted butter

1 cup (240 ml) marshmallow crème

1 to 2 tablespoons milk

Make the cookies: Sift the flour, cocoa powder, baking soda, baking powder, and salt into a large bowl. In another large bowl, beat the sugar and butter with an electric mixer on medium-high speed until light and fluffy, about 5 minutes. Add the egg and beat until incorporated. Beat in the vanilla. Alternate adding the flour mixture and the milk, beginning and ending with the flour mixture. Mix until just incorporated. Refrigerate the dough until chilled, about 1 hour.

Adjust the oven racks to the top and bottom thirds of the oven and preheat to 400°F (205°C). Line two baking sheets with parchment paper and lightly coat with cooking spray.

Drop tablespoonfuls of batter about 3 inches (7.5 cm) apart on the prepared sheets, about 6 cookies per baking sheet. Keep the remaining batter chilled while working.

Bake until the cookies puff up, about 7 minutes. Let cool on the pans for a few minutes, then transfer to a wire rack to cool completely. Let the baking sheets cool, reline with parchment, spray, and bake the remaining batter in batches.

Make the filling: Beat the confectioners' sugar and butter in a large bowl with an electric mixer on medium speed until fluffy. Add the marshmallow crème and milk and beat until light and airy, about 5 minutes.

Spread a heaping tablespoon of the filling onto half of the cookies. Sandwich with the remaining halves, pushing down slightly. Store in an airtight container.

Miso Chocolate Chunk Cookies

YIELD
24 to 30 cookies
servings

ACTIVE TIME
15 minutes

TOTAL TIME
1 hour 40 minutes

If I could only choose one dessert (besides frozen yogurt) to eat for the rest of my life, it would be warm chocolate chip cookies straight from the oven with a glass of milk. I am always trying to perfect my recipe. I like a chewy chocolate chip cookie, none of these flat, crispy cookies for me. Give me the chew and make it soft. I know it sounds weird, but white miso paste is *the* secret ingredient for the perfect cookie. You don't taste miso, but the umami makes the chocolate even more chocolaty and gives the cookie a chewier texture. Trust.

1 cup (220 g) lightly packed light brown sugar

3 tablespoons granulated sugar

½ cup (1 stick/115 g) unsalted butter, at room temperature

1 large egg

⅓ cup (75 ml) white miso paste

1 teaspoon vanilla extract

2 cups (255 g) all-purpose flour

1 teaspoon baking soda

1½ cups (255 g) semisweet chocolate chunks

Beat both sugars and the butter together in a medium bowl with an electric mixer until creamy. Add the egg, miso paste, and vanilla and beat until well mixed. Add the flour and baking soda and mix until just combined. Stir in the chocolate chunks. Cover with plastic wrap and refrigerate for at least 1 hour (this is very important in order to have a chewy cookie that doesn't spread out too much).

Preheat the oven to 350°F (175°C). Spray two baking sheets with nonstick cooking spray.

Use a medium ice cream scoop to portion cookie dough onto the prepared pans. Use two fingers to lightly flatten each scoop of dough. Bake, rotating and switching the pans halfway through, 13 to 14 minutes for a chewy cookie (a few minutes longer if you like a more well-done cookie). Transfer to a wire rack to cool (though I usually eat one straight out of the oven!).

Mango Dump Cake

YIELD
8 servings

ACTIVE TIME
10 minutes

TOTAL TIME
1 hour 10 minutes

Dump cake may not be the prettiest name, or even the prettiest cake, for that matter, but it sure does taste good (and that's really all that matters IMHO!). There are many great things about a dump cake: It's easy, it lends itself to last-minute baking, and it's versatile. You can use just about any frozen fruit and any flavor of cake mix. Top it with ice cream and voilà, you've got a delish dessert.

Two 12-ounce (340 g) bags frozen mango chunks, thawed

1 (15¼ ounce [432 g]) box yellow cake mix

½ cup (1 stick/115 g) unsalted butter, melted

Coconut ice cream, for serving

½ cup (45 g) sweetened shredded coconut

Preheat the oven to 350°F (175°C). Grease a 9 by 13-inch (23 by 33 cm) baking dish with nonstick cooking spray.

Put the mango in the prepared baking dish. Evenly distribute the cake mix over the mango. Drizzle the butter evenly over the entire dish. Bake until firm and golden brown, about 55 minutes.

Spread the coconut in a baking dish and toast in the oven until golden brown, about 5 minutes.

Serve the cake with coconut ice cream and toasted coconut.

Cannoli Trifle

YIELD
8 to 10 servings

TOTAL TIME
30 minutes

Ryan and I took a trip to Sicily last summer, and I made it my mission to try as many cannoli as possible. He's not as hot on them as I am, but he still joined in on the fun. I think the best was at a small bakery, tucked in a side street in Taormina. I actually don't need to travel far to get my number-one cannoli, though; it's right here in New York City at my all-time favorite restaurant, Emilio's Ballato. What I love the most about a cannoli is the filling, all that creamy ricotta and chocolate chips, with just a touch of orange. I decided to try making a cannoli trifle after having a cannoli cake and the results were A+. Try making this for a dinner party or to take along the next time you're invited to someone's house. The longer it sits, the better it gets, so you can make it in advance and everyone will swoon.

One 15¼-ounce (432 g) box yellow cake mix, mixed and baked according to package instructions for a 9 by 13-inch (23 by 33 cm) cake

2 tablespoons orange liqueur, such as Cointreau

3 cups (720 ml) heavy cream

¾ cup (95 g) confectioners' sugar

1 pound (455 g) fresh ricotta

2 cups (370 g) mini chocolate chips

1 teaspoon vanilla extract

2 cups (255 g) toasted, chopped pistachios

Brush the baked cake with the orange liqueur. Set aside to soak in while you make the filling.

Beat the cream and confectioners' sugar to soft peaks with an electric mixer. Reserve 2 cups (480 ml) of the whipped cream for the top of the trifle.

In a large bowl, mix the ricotta, vanilla, and 1 cup (185 g) of the chocolate chips in a large bowl. Fold in the whipped cream until well combined. Crumble or cube the soaked cake into large pieces. Spoon or pipe one-third of the filling into the bottom of a trifle or serving dish. Sprinkle one-quarter of the pistachios over the filling, then top with one-third of the cake. Repeat the layers twice more with the remaining ingredients, finishing with the filling and reserving ½ cup (65 g) of the pistachios for topping. Top the trifle with the reserved whipped cream. Cover and chill for at least 4 hours or overnight. When ready to serve, sprinkle with the reserved pistachios and the remaining 1 cup chocolate chips. Serve chilled.

Apple Cobbler

YIELD
8 servings

ACTIVE TIME
15 minutes

TOTAL TIME
1 hour 5 minutes

Every summer, I wait for peaches to come in season so I can make peach cobbler. I use my grandma's recipe, which features an unusual process (you'll see what I mean when you read it through). I started thinking, why do I only make this cobbler with peaches? So I started using the same method to make berry cobblers and eventually apple cobbler. I add cinnamon to the apples (I do not add it to other fruit versions), and when I want a little extra zip I stir in some bourbon.

4 cups (435 g) sliced apples, peel left on (about 5 apples)

1 teaspoon ground cinnamon

1¼ cups (250 g) sugar

1 tablespoon bourbon (optional)

1 cup (125 g) all-purpose flour

1 teaspoon baking powder

1 teaspoon kosher salt

½ cup (120 ml) milk

4 tablespoons (55 g) unsalted butter, melted

1 tablespoon cornstarch

½ cup (120 ml) boiling water

Vanilla ice cream and caramel sauce, for serving

Preheat the oven to 350°F (175°C).

Put the apples in a 9-inch (23 cm) square baking dish. Toss with the cinnamon, ¼ cup (50 g) of the sugar, and the bourbon, if using. Set aside.

In a medium bowl, combine the flour, ¾ cup (150 g) of the sugar, the baking powder, and ½ teaspoon of the salt. Add the milk and butter and mix until just combined. Pour the batter evenly over the apples.

In a small bowl, mix the remaining ¼ cup (50 g) sugar, the cornstarch, and remaining ½ teaspoon salt. Sprinkle the mixture over the batter. Evenly pour the boiling water all over.

Bake until golden brown and bubbling, 45 to 50 minutes. Serve warm with ice cream and drizzled with caramel sauce.

Affogato

Essentially, an affogato is an Italian dessert that is just a scoop of vanilla ice cream with a shot of espresso poured over it. Pretty much the simplest dessert ever! Here are a few combos that put a spin on the classic.

Salted caramel ice cream
with espresso

Lemon sorbet with limoncello

Chocolate ice cream with
hazelnut liqueur

Butter pecan ice cream with
ginger liqueur

Chocolate ice cream with
orange liqueur

Chocolate Pudding

I used to beg my mom to make chocolate pudding for me for dessert. She didn't really use a recipe, she would just wing it each time, so sometimes it would be more chocolaty than others. Contrary to what pudding "should" be like, I wanted it to be lumpy. I don't know why, I guess I just liked that texture. Mom's technique was to thicken with cornstarch, and, unlike with most pudding recipes, she never put egg yolks into it. This method eliminates the step of having to temper the egg yolks, so it cuts down on time and effort (which I am always a fan of!). I make mine much more rich than my mom did, so if you like yours lighter, cut the cocoa powder down to ¾ cup.

1 cup (95 g) cocoa powder

1 cup (200 g) sugar

3 tablespoons cornstarch

½ teaspoon kosher salt

4 cups (945 ml) whole milk

1½ teaspoons vanilla extract

In a large saucepan set over medium heat, combine the cocoa, sugar, cornstarch, and salt and mix well. Whisk in the milk. Stir constantly with a wooden spoon while the mixture comes to a low boil and begins to thicken, 5 to 6 minutes. Reduce the heat to low. Stir constantly as the mixture continues to thicken to the consistency of pudding, another 7 to 8 minutes.

Remove from the heat and stir in the vanilla. Place plastic wrap directly on the surface of the pudding to prevent a skin from forming, and then cool to room temperature. Refrigerate until chilled, 2 to 3 hours. I like to serve this spooned into teacups with a dollop of whipped cream.

Stone Fruit Crisp

YIELD
8 to 10 servings

ACTIVE TIME
10 minutes

TOTAL TIME
1 hour 5 minutes

I look forward to summer stone fruits all year long. Peach is my number one, but I also love a ripe plum, especially when the flesh is bright red, or a juicy apricot on a hot summer day. Any of these fruits would work well on their own in this crisp, but the combination of the three is like a celebration of the season. Be sure to serve this hot out of the oven, with a scoop of vanilla ice cream!

For the crisp:

½ cup (65 g) all-purpose flour

¼ cup (55 g) light brown sugar

Pinch of ground cinnamon

Pinch of kosher salt

½ cup (1 stick/115 g) cold unsalted butter, cut into cubes

½ cup (45 g) rolled oats

For the fruit:

4 peaches, sliced

2 plums, sliced

2 apricots, sliced

3 teaspoons cornstarch

¼ cup (50 g) sugar

Preheat the oven to 400°F (205°C).

Make the crisp: Mix together the flour, brown sugar, cinnamon, and salt in a bowl. Using a pastry blender, two knives, or a food processor, cut in the butter. Stir in the oats.

Prepare the fruit: Toss the fruit with the cornstarch and sugar.

Transfer the fruit mixture to a 9 by 13-inch baking dish and top with the crisp mixture. Bake until the middle is warmed through and the top is crispy and golden brown, 50 to 55 minutes.

Brioche
French Toast
Casserole
194

Eggs in
Purgatory
196

6, 8, 10 Boiled Eggs
197

Brown Sugar and
Sriracha Bacon
197

Breakfast
Nachos
198

Pineapple
Green Smoothie
200

Banana Coffee
Smoothie
200

Smoothie
Bowls
201

Molasses Spiced
Monkey Bread
203

Basil Zucchini
Frittata
204

Blackberry
Cornbread Muffins
205

Fluffy Pancakes
206

Simple Scrambled
Eggs with Chives
208

Mom's Granola
209

Drop Biscuits
211

Berry Quinoa
Porridge
212

Backpack Bagel
213

Coconut
Banana Bread
215

chapter six

———

BREAKFASTS AND BRUNCHES

Brioche French Toast Casserole

YIELD

4 to 6 servings

TOTAL TIME

1 hour 10 minutes

Breakfast wins the award for Meal Most Likely to Make You Feel like a Short Order Cook. If you have a house full of people, or friends coming for brunch, make this Brioche French Toast Casserole. You can completely assemble it ahead of time (even the night before) and bake it just before serving. Brioche is buttery and decadent on its own, so when soaked in this custard and baked, then topped with berries, confectioners' sugar, and maple syrup, it is totally off the charts.

1 loaf brioche, cut into ½-inch (12 mm) slices

4 large eggs, lightly beaten

2 cups (480 ml) milk

¼ cup (50 g) granulated sugar

1 teaspoon vanilla extract

½ teaspoon ground cinnamon

Zest and juice of 1 lemon

Pinch of kosher salt

1 cup (145 g) fresh blueberries

Confectioners' sugar and maple syrup, for serving

Preheat the oven to 350°F (175°C). Butter a 9 by 13-inch (23 by 33 cm) baking dish.

Arrange the brioche slices in the baking dish, shingling them to overlap slightly. Whisk together the eggs, milk, granulated sugar, vanilla, cinnamon, lemon zest and juice, and salt, then gently stir in the blueberries. Pour the mixture over the bread, making sure the berries are evenly distributed. Let the mixture soak into the bread at room temperature for 30 minutes. Bake for 35 to 40 minutes, until the egg is set and the bread starts to brown. Remove from the oven and let cool for a couple of minutes before serving. Scoop out a portion and top with confectioners' sugar and maple syrup.

Eggs in Purgatory

YIELD
4 to 6 servings

TOTAL TIME
35 to 55 minutes

This is inspired by a classic Italian breakfast dish. It is called "purgatory" because the spicy, bubbly tomato sauce is meant to mimic the fires of hell. Kinda morbid, but it really is much more heavenly than it sounds! If you have leftover marinara sauce, this is a great way to use it. I also like this dish as a "breakfast for dinner" option.

1 tablespoon extra-virgin olive oil

½ yellow onion, thinly sliced

½ red bell pepper, thinly sliced

1 Fresno chile, minced

2½ cups (600 ml) marinara sauce (homemade or your favorite jarred)

6 to 8 large eggs

Kosher salt and freshly ground black pepper

Freshly grated Pecorino Romano cheese

Minced fresh flat-leaf parsley

Toasted crusty bread, for serving

Heat the oil in a large skillet over medium heat. Add the onion, bell pepper, and chile and sauté until tender, 8 to 10 minutes. Stir in the sauce and bring to a low simmer. Using a spoon, and working one at a time, create a well in the sauce and crack an egg into it. Sprinkle each egg with salt and pepper. Reduce the heat to low, cover, and cook until the eggs are the desired doneness, about 10 to 12 minutes for a runny egg, 12 to 14 minutes for medium, and 16 to 18 for well-done. Serve topped with cheese and parsley, with toasted crusty bread.

6, 8, 10 Boiled Eggs

YIELD
6 servings

TOTAL TIME
10 minutes

Boiled eggs are one of those things that are so simple, they end up being tricky. I think it is best to bring the water to a boil, then lower the egg into the water. It creates a vacuum, and the eggs will be easier to peel. For a loose, soft-boiled egg, cook for 6 minutes. If you like the yolk to be more cooked and only slightly jammy, then go for 8 minutes. Ten minutes will give you a firm egg, but it will still be bright yellow, and still soft. Use the timer on your phone instead of trying to guess or, if you're like me, 20 minutes will have gone by and you'll have completely forgotten you were even boiling eggs.

6 large eggs

Kosher salt and cracked black pepper

Bring 2 quarts (2 L) of water to a boil. Carefully lower the eggs into the water. Lower the heat to medium for a slow rolling boil. Set a timer for 6, 8, or 10 minutes. Prepare a water bath with ice. When the timer goes off, transfer the eggs carefully to the ice bath. Peel the eggs once they are cool to the touch and serve.

Brown Sugar and Sriracha Bacon

YIELD
4 to 6 servings

TOTAL TIME
15 minutes

As if bacon isn't good enough on its own, let's add sugar and spice. Now it's truly everything nice. (Sorry, I'm corny and I couldn't resist!) This bacon is great for breakfast or brunch, but I also love it as a cocktail-hour snack or even as a garnish for a Bloody Mary. You can also try substituting sambal or harissa for the sriracha, or if those are too spicy for you, just use Dijon mustard.

10 slices regular-cut bacon (thick-cut won't crisp up enough)

3 tablespoons dark brown sugar

2 tablespoons sriracha

Preheat the oven to 400°F (205°C). Line a rimmed baking sheet with parchment paper and top with a wire rack. Spray with nonstick cooking spray.

In a medium bowl, combine the brown sugar and sriracha. Mix well. Add the bacon and toss to coat. Transfer the bacon to the wire rack. Bake for 12 minutes, until browned and crispy. Let cool slightly, then serve.

Breakfast Nachos

YIELD
6 servings

ACTIVE TIME
20 minutes

TOTAL TIME
30 minutes

These nachos are pretty much insane. They're kind of a breakfast hash-nacho mash-up, and I'm here for it. These are really fun to share with friends or if you just feel like having a super-indulgent weekend breakfast with the family. I advise that you don't plan to do much of anything afterward, because you're probably gonna want to hit the couch for a bit.

One 20 ounce (567 g) bag frozen sweet potato waffle fries

1 pound (455 g) breakfast sausage, casings removed and meat crumbled

1 tablespoon olive oil

6 large eggs

Kosher salt and freshly ground black pepper

1 tablespoon maple syrup

2 cups (225 g) shredded sharp cheddar cheese

1 avocado, thinly sliced

½ cup (90 g) quartered cherry tomatoes

3 scallions, white and light green parts, thinly sliced

1 jalapeño, thinly sliced

¼ cup (10 g) chopped fresh cilantro

Sour cream

Hot sauce (optional)

Preheat the oven to 350°F (175°C).

Spread the fries onto a rimmed baking sheet and bake according to the package instructions.

Meanwhile, cook the sausage in a large nonstick skillet over medium-high heat, breaking up any big chunks with the back of a wooden spoon, until browned and cooked through, about 5 minutes.

Heat another large nonstick skillet over medium heat. Swirl in the oil. Crack the eggs into individual bowls. Add the eggs side by side in the pan. Cook until the outer edges turn opaque, about 1 minute, then cover, lower the heat, and cook for 4 minutes. If you want a medium yolk, cook for 5 minutes. Season with salt and pepper to taste.

When the fries are ready, turn the oven to broil. Top the fries with the sausage and cover with the cheese. Cook under the broiler until the cheese has melted completely, about 2 minutes.

Top the nachos with the cooked eggs, avocado slices, tomatoes, scallions, jalapeño, and cilantro. Dollop with sour cream and serve with hot sauce, if desired.

Pineapple Green Smoothie

This is one of my go-to breakfast smoothies, and I'll also have it for an afternoon pick-me-up. The frozen banana and pineapple whips up into a creamy concoction that is more like ice cream, and the spinach is undetectable in flavor, only present in color. The mint adds this punch of freshness that just says, "Today is gonna be a good day!"

YIELD
1 serving

TOTAL TIME
5 minutes

1 frozen banana

½ cup (10 g) spinach

1 cup (165 g) frozen pineapple pieces

2 to 3 fresh mint leaves

½ cup (120 ml) almond milk

1 scoop vanilla protein powder (optional)

Put all the ingredients in a blender and blend until completely smooth. Serve immediately.

Banana Coffee Smoothie

This is the ultimate I'm-in-a-hurry-and-trying-to-get-to-work smoothie. It's coffee and breakfast all in one, and what's not to love about the flavor combo of banana, chocolate, and coffee? More like a milkshake than a smoothie, in my opinion. If you want to pump it up even more, add a scoop of your favorite vanilla or chocolate protein powder.

YIELD
1 serving

TOTAL TIME
5 minutes

1 frozen banana

½ cup (120 ml) almond milk

¼ cup (60 ml) brewed espresso, cooled

2 tablespoons raw almonds

1 tablespoon semisweet chocolate chips (or, for less sweet, 1 tablespoon cacao nibs or cocoa powder)

Handful of ice

Put all the ingredients in a blender and blend until completely smooth. Serve immediately.

Smoothie Bowls

YIELD

2 to 4 servings

TOTAL TIME

5 minutes

Ryan and I eat a smoothie bowl pretty much every single morning. I buy large bags of frozen fruit and we dump it all in the blender. We have a basket labeled "smoothies" in the cabinet that has all of our toppings so we can just pull it out and have everything in one place. I like starting my day with this antioxidant, fiber-rich punch.

½ cup (85 g) frozen chopped pineapple

½ cup (85 g) frozen chopped mango

½ cup (80 g) frozen blueberries

½ cup (75 g) frozen strawberries

2 bananas

½ cup (120 ml) almond or soy milk, or desired milk

¼ cup (60 ml) orange juice

Toppings: sliced banana, granola, chia seeds, goji berries, peanut butter, and bee pollen

Put the pineapple, mango, blueberries, strawberries, bananas, milk, and orange juice in a blender. Start on low, then move to high speed and blend until totally pureed. Serve in a bowl topped with sliced banana, granola, chia seeds, goji berries, peanut butter, and bee pollen.

Molasses Spiced Monkey Bread

YIELD
8 servings

ACTIVE TIME
25 minutes

TOTAL TIME
55 to 65 minutes
(includes cooling
time)

I first had monkey bread when I was a freshman in high school and I went to a sleepover at my friend Erica's house. Erica's mom, Diane, was known for her sweet tea (it was sweeeeeeet) and she would also make monkey bread for slumber parties. Her recipe was the classic cinnamon and sugar combo, and we would sit in Erica's basement, picking at the monkey bread and gossiping about boys. I've made it several different ways throughout the years and this molasses spice rendition is one of my favorites. It is ooey and gooey and perfect with a cup of coffee. I serve it when I have house guests, so I guess you could say it is still a slumber-party staple.

1 tablespoon ground cinnamon

1 teaspoon ground ginger

¼ teaspoon grated nutmeg

⅛ teaspoon ground cloves

⅛ teaspoon kosher salt

¼ cup (55 g) unsalted butter

¾ cup (165 g) packed brown sugar

¼ cup (60 ml) molasses

1 teaspoon orange zest

½ cup (100 g) granulated sugar

Two 16.3-ounce (462 g) cans biscuit dough, biscuits cut into quarters and rolled into balls

Preheat the oven to 350°F (175°C). Spray a 12-cup (2.8 L) Bundt pan with nonstick cooking spray.

In a small bowl, combine the cinnamon, ginger, nutmeg, cloves, and salt.

Melt the butter in a saucepan, then whisk in the brown sugar, molasses, orange zest, and 2 teaspoons of the spice mixture until smooth. Remove from the heat.

Mix the granulated sugar and remaining spice mixture in a large bowl. Add the biscuit dough balls and toss in the sugar-spice mixture to coat.

Spread one-third of the molasses mixture in the bottom of the prepared Bundt pan. Arrange half of the biscuit pieces on top, then layer in another third of the molasses mixture. Top with the remaining biscuit pieces, then the remaining molasses mixture. Bake until browned on top, 35 to 45 minutes. Allow to cool on a rack for 15 minutes. Invert the monkey bread onto a plate and serve.

Basil Zucchini Frittata

YIELD
4 to 6 servings

TOTAL TIME
35 minutes

Let me tell you, this frittata is beyond. During the summer, when zucchini is abundant, I'm always looking for ways to use it. When spiralizers became all the rage, I jumped right on board the trend, but after a few meals of spiralized zucchini with tomato sauce, I was bored. That spiralizer I had to have became my latest dust collector. So I got to thinking, what else could I use this thing for? I kept the zucchini theme here, but I was inspired by the Italian frittatas that use leftover spaghetti. It's important to sauté the zucchini first so it releases its water content, then add in the other ingredients. This frittata is good hot out of the oven, at room temperature, or straight out of the fridge the next day.

12 large eggs

½ cup (50 g) grated Parmesan cheese

1½ teaspoons kosher salt

1 teaspoon cracked black pepper

2 tablespoons extra-virgin olive oil

1 shallot, minced

4 zucchini, spiralized, ribboned, or very thinly sliced

4 tablespoons (10 g) fresh basil, cut into chiffonade

Preheat the oven to 375°F (190°C).

Whisk the eggs, ¼ cup (25 g) of the cheese, ½ teaspoon of the salt, and ½ teaspoon of the pepper in a large bowl.

Heat the oil in a 12-inch (30.5 cm) cast-iron skillet and add the shallot. Cook for 4 to 5 minutes, until very soft. Add the zucchini, the remaining 1 teaspoon salt, and ½ teaspoon pepper and cook for 5 to 6 minutes, until the zucchini releases its liquid. Pour in the egg mixture, sprinkle with 2 tablespoons of the basil, and stir to distribute the zucchini and basil into the eggs. Let cook for 2 to 3 minutes on the stovetop, then transfer to the oven and bake for 15 to 20 minutes, until very fluffy and set in the middle. Sprinkle with the remaining cheese and basil. Serve warm or at room temperature.

Blackberry Cornbread Muffins

YIELD
12 muffins

ACTIVE TIME
10 minutes

TOTAL TIME
25 to 27 minutes,
plus cooling time

At my grandparents' house, we had homemade cornbread every single night. Either my grandpa or my grandma would make it. They'd heat up an iron skillet in the oven, then pour the cornbread batter into it. It would sizzle, setting that crispy crust almost instantly. I loved it. My grandpa would always have an additional piece for dessert with butter and molasses. Years ago, I took his idea of having cornbread as dessert and used it as an alternative to shortcake. I served hot sliced cornbread with a fresh blackberry compote and whipped cream. Yum! That idea evolved into these muffins. Eat them hot out of the oven with a big schmear of butter. And if you have molasses, try them grandpa-style.

1½ cups (270 g) fine-ground cornmeal

1½ cups (190 g) plus 2 teaspoons all-purpose flour

2 tablespoons baking powder

1 teaspoon kosher salt

2 cups (480 ml) buttermilk

1 cup (200 g) sugar

2 large eggs

½ cup (120 ml) vegetable oil

1 teaspoon vanilla extract

1 cup (145 g) corn kernels (cut fresh from the cob, if possible, or thawed if frozen)

1½ cups (215 g) fresh blackberries

Preheat the oven to 400°F (205°C). Spray a 12-cup muffin tin with nonstick cooking spray.

In a large bowl, combine the cornmeal, 1½ cups (270 g) flour, the baking powder, and salt.

In a medium bowl, whisk the buttermilk, sugar, eggs, oil, and vanilla until smooth.

Add the buttermilk mixture and the corn to the cornmeal mixture and stir until just combined. Do not overmix. Toss the blackberries with the remaining 2 teaspoons flour. Gently fold the blackberries into the batter.

Use an ice cream scoop to portion the batter into the muffin tin. Bake until golden brown and a cake tester comes out clean, 15 to 17 minutes. Cool on a wire rack. Store in an airtight container for 4 to 5 days.

Fluffy Pancakes

YIELD
4 to 6 servings

TOTAL TIME
40 minutes

My grandma made big breakfasts on Saturday and Sunday mornings. One day would be biscuits, the other pancakes. She would coat the griddle in butter, which not only gave the pancakes that undeniable buttery goodness, but also got them nice and crispy on the edges. I like my pancakes to be as fluffy as possible. I started separating the eggs and whipping the whites to give them volume, and it's so worth the extra step. Also worth the extra time: letting the batter rest for 20 minutes before you cook it. This will guarantee you a fluffier pancake every time.

2 large eggs, separated

1½ cups (190 g) all-purpose flour

2 tablespoons sugar

2 tablespoons baking powder

¼ teaspoon kosher salt

1½ cups (360 ml) milk

2 tablespoons unsalted butter, melted, plus more for the skillet

Beat the egg whites to stiff peaks in a large bowl with an electric mixer.

In a separate bowl, whisk together the flour, sugar, baking powder, and salt. Pour in the milk, egg yolks, and melted butter and whisk until combined and mostly smooth—there might be a few lumps. Gently fold in egg whites. Cover the batter and refrigerate for 20 minutes.

Melt 2 tablespoons butter in a large skillet over medium heat. Using a ladle or a measuring cup, pour out 3 pancakes, about ¼ cup (60 ml) of batter apiece. Cook until bubbles form in the middle of the batter, 3 to 4 minutes. Flip and cook on the other side for another 3 minutes. Repeat with the remaining batter, adding more butter if the pan dries out. Serve warm.

Simple Scrambled Eggs with Chives

If you've ever been to France, or ordered scrambled eggs in a French restaurant, you know they do them right. The key is to cook them low and slow. Butter certainly helps as well. I like to sprinkle in some fresh chives and to serve them with toast (and more butter). Stir in a little cheese at the end, if that's your jam.

YIELD
4 servings

TOTAL TIME
15 minutes

8 large eggs

½ teaspoon kosher salt

2 tablespoons unsalted butter

2 tablespoons chopped fresh chives

Whisk together the eggs and salt.

Melt the butter in a cast-iron or nonstick skillet over medium-low heat, then add the eggs. Stir constantly; when curds start to form, reduce the heat to low. Cook for 15 to 18 minutes, stirring constantly, until the eggs are cooked but still a little wet. Sprinkle the chives over the top and serve.

Mom's Granola

YIELD
About 7½ to 8 cups

ACTIVE TIME
10 minutes

TOTAL TIME
50 minutes, plus
cooling time

My mom is known in her town for her granola. She sells it at her local farmers' market, The Wild Ramp, in Huntington, West Virginia. They sell out as soon as she brings it in and are always asking for more. I have told her she needs to raise her price! I like that it is lower in sugar and easy to make adjustments according to your tastes and what you have on hand. Use any combination of nuts you like.

3½ cups old-fashioned rolled oats

½ cup unsalted sunflower seeds

½ cup unsalted pumpkin seeds

1 cup unsweetened flaked coconut

1½ cups unsalted chopped nuts

½ teaspoon salt

½ cup extra-virgin olive oil

½ cup pure maple syrup

½ cup chopped dried fruit

Preheat the oven to 250°F (120°C). Line two large baking sheets with parchment paper.

In a large bowl, mix the oats, seeds, coconut, nuts, and salt. Add the olive oil and maple syrup. Stir until all ingredients are evenly coated. Divide the mixture onto the two prepared baking sheets and use the back of a wooden spoon to spread the mixture evenly in the pans. Bake for 35 to 40 minutes. Let cool to room temperature.

Pick up the opposite edges of the parchment paper and transfer into a large bowl. Stir in the dried fruit. Transfer to airtight containers. Keeps up to 1 month.

Drop Biscuits

YIELD
12 biscuits

ACTIVE TIME
25 minutes

TOTAL TIME
45 minutes

We had biscuits almost every weekend at my grandparents' house when I was a kid. I couldn't get enough of them. My grandma always let me help, and I so enjoyed rolling out the dough and using the biscuit cutter. Drop biscuits are kind of a shortcut biscuit, in that you don't have to take the steps of rolling them out and cutting them. Just mix the dough and drop them one by one onto a baking pan. I like to add different flavorings to them as well, like garlic cheddar (if you've ever been to a certain seafood chain restaurant, you know what I'm talking about). Just add 1 teaspoon of garlic powder to the dry ingredients and 1 ½ cups grated cheese and 2 tablespoons minced parsley when mixing in the butter and buttermilk. I also substitute grated Gruyère and tarragon, which is really tasty, and you can use these drop biscuits as a crust when making a pot pie.

2 cups (255 g) all-purpose flour

1 tablespoon baking powder

1 tablespoon sugar

½ teaspoon kosher salt

½ cup (1 stick/115 g) unsalted butter, cut into small cubes and chilled, plus 2 tablespoons melted

1¼ cups (300 ml) buttermilk

Flaky sea salt

Preheat the oven to 450°F (230°C). Coat a baking sheet with nonstick cooking spray.

Whisk together the flour, baking powder, sugar, and kosher salt in a large bowl. Add the chilled butter and use a pastry cutter or two knives to blend until the mixture resembles a coarse meal. Make a well in the mixture and add the buttermilk, then stir until just combined.

Use a large ice cream scoop to drop biscuits onto the prepared baking sheet. Use a pastry brush to lightly brush the tops with the melted butter. Sprinkle with flaky sea salt. Bake until golden brown, 15 to 18 minutes. Serve immediately.

Berry Quinoa Porridge

I like starting my day with some kind of fruit, whether it's a fruit bowl, a smoothie, or just a handful of berries in a bowl of cereal. By blending berries into the milk, then cooking the quinoa in it, you get a big boost of antioxidants, plus a healthy dose of fiber and protein from the grain. This is a warm, comforting, and healthy way to start the day. It reheats beautifully, so keep it in the fridge and heat up a portion each morning.

YIELD
4 servings

TOTAL TIME
30 minutes

3 cups (720 ml) almond milk, or your favorite alternative milk

1 cup (170 g) white quinoa, rinsed and drained

½ vanilla bean, split and scraped

Pinch of kosher salt

2 cups (290 g) mixed berries (raspberries, strawberries, blueberries)

½ teaspoon ground cinnamon

3 tablespoons honey

Toppings: sliced banana, sliced almonds, chia seeds, cacao nibs, dried fruit, or your favorite porridge toppings

Heat 1 cup (240 ml) of the almond milk, 1 cup (240 ml) water, the quinoa, vanilla bean (seeds and pod), and salt in a medium saucepan over medium heat. Bring to a boil, then turn heat to low, cover, and simmer for 15 minutes, or until the quinoa is tender and the liquid is absorbed.

While the quinoa cooks, put the berries, cinnamon, honey, and remaining 2 cups (480 ml) almond milk in a blender. Blend until mostly smooth (or leave chunks of berries if you want!). Add to the cooked quinoa and simmer, stirring occasionally, for another 15 minutes, or until the porridge is warm and thickened. Remove and discard the vanilla bean pod. Serve immediately with your favorite toppings or refrigerate until ready to serve and reheat with a little water or almond milk.

Backpack Bagel

YIELD
1 serving

TOTAL TIME
5 minutes

I went to college at Miami University in Ohio. (For those scratching their heads at that, Miami was a university before Florida was a state.) We had a great breakfast spot called Uptown Bakery, and when I wanted to treat myself, I'd walk up there and get a Backpack Bagel. I still think about those mornings with my girlfriends, drinking our coffee and enjoying our bagels.

1 whole wheat bagel, split and toasted

¼ cup (60 ml) creamy peanut butter

½ Granny Smith apple, thinly sliced

¼ cup (30 g) granola

1 teaspoon chia seeds

Spread the peanut butter onto both halves of the bagel. Top the peanut butter with shingled slices of apple, then the granola and chia seeds. Serve.

Coconut Banana Bread

YIELD
8 servings

ACTIVE TIME
25 minutes

TOTAL TIME
1 hour 15 minutes to
1 hour 25 minutes

Banana bread has always been my jam. I can't turn it down. My grandma made the absolute best; I would take it to school with me, and all of my friends would go nuts for it. A few years ago, I went on a trip to Jamaica, and the hotel where I stayed served banana coconut pancakes. The other day, I had a bunch of ripe bananas and was getting ready to make a loaf of Grandma's classic, and then for some reason I started thinking about those pancakes. So I thought, why not combine the two? In a twist of fate, I called my mom just as I was about to make the banana bread and told her my plan. She said that Grandma actually used to make a coconut banana bread, and she would put lime in it. And get this: She called it "Jamaican banana bread"! It was a sign. By the way, pretty sure my grandma never went to Jamaica.

For the banana bread:

2 cups (255 g) all-purpose flour

¾ teaspoon baking soda

½ teaspoon baking powder

½ teaspoon kosher salt

3 very ripe bananas, lightly mashed

2 large eggs, lightly beaten

1 cup (200 g) sugar

½ cup (120 ml) coconut oil

½ cup (120 ml) coconut milk

1 teaspoon vanilla extract

Zest of 1 lime

¼ cup (55 g) lightly packed sweetened shredded coconut

For the topping:

3 tablespoons sweetened shredded coconut

2 tablespoons dark brown sugar

Juice of 1 lime

Make the banana bread: Preheat the oven to 350°F (175°C). Coat a 9 × 5 × 3-inch loaf pan with nonstick cooking spray and place it on a baking sheet.

Sift the flour, baking soda, baking powder, and salt together into a medium bowl.

In a large bowl, use an electric mixer to combine the bananas, eggs, sugar, oil, coconut milk, vanilla, and lime zest. Beat until creamy, 2 to 3 minutes. Stir in the coconut. Add the flour mixture and use a wooden spoon or rubber spatula to mix until just combined, taking care to not overmix. Transfer to the prepared loaf pan. Bake for 50 to 60 minutes, until golden brown and a cake tester or toothpick comes out clean from the center. Let cool in the pan for about 10 minutes.

In the meantime, make the topping: In a small saucepan, combine the coconut, brown sugar, and lime juice. Bring to a simmer and cook until reduced to a syrup, 1 to 2 minutes.

Remove the banana bread to a cooling rack. Spoon the coconut mixture on top. Let cool, slice, and serve.

ACKNOWLEDGMENTS

This book was a true journey, and I could not have made it to the finish line without a great team. Thank you to Lucy Schaeffer for your beautiful photography and Mariana Velasquez for your stunning work styling the recipes. Martha Bernarbe, thank you for capturing my vision with your beautiful props. Thank you to Martha Tinkler for all your help testing these recipes to ensure that they work for my readers.

This is my second cookbook with Abrams, and I am so grateful to everyone there. To Deb Wood for the lovely design and Shawn Dahl for managing the design process so seamlessly. To Lisa Silverman, managing editor extraordinaire, and to Sarah Scheffel and Liana Krissoff, for their copyediting and proofreading, and Sarah Masterson Halley, who oversaw the book's proofing and production: Thank you for your attention to detail. Last but certainly not least, a gigantic thank-you to my editor, Holly Dolce, whom I can always count on not only to talk recipes, but to share a good laugh about early motherhood trials and tribulations.

Thank you to David Larabell, my agent at CAA, and to Leslie Sloane, Jami Kandel, and Jessica Pierson, my publicists at Vision PR.

And to my favorite taste tester, my husband, Ryan, thank you.

acorn squash
  Roasted Red Curry
      Acorn Squash, 161
Affogato, 186, *187*
almond milk, 200, 212
almonds, *44*, 45
  Spicy Kale Caesar with
      Crispy Onions,
      Almonds, Avocado,
      and Croutons,
      52, 53
  Swiss Chard with
      Almonds and
      Raisins, 165
Amalfi Spritz, 12, 15, *15*
Animal-Style Burgers,
    110, 111
apples, *184*
  Apple Cobbler, 185
  Bagel, Backpack, 213
apricots/apricot jam
  Apricot-Glazed Ham,
      117
  Stone Fruit Crisp, 190,
      191
artichoke hearts
  Creamy Spinach
      Artichoke Pasta,
      78, *79*
  Crispy Artichoke
      Hearts, 29
arugula, *134*, 135
  Arugula, Fennel, and
      Citrus Salad, 43
  Grilled Sweet Potato
      and Arugula Salad,
      42
  Pesto Farro with
      Smoked
      Mozzarella,
      Arugula, Corn, and
      Tomatoes, 54, *55*
avocado, 35, *36–37*
  Lobster Cobb, 58, *59*

Spicy Kale Caesar with
    Crispy Onions,
    Almonds, Avocado,
    and Croutons,
    52, 53

———

bacon
  Brown Sugar and
      Sriracha Bacon,
      197
  Grilled Farmers'
      Market "Paella,"
      138, *139*
  Iceberg Disk Salad,
      40, *41*
  Lobster Cobb, 58, *59*
  Peach, Bourbon, and
      Bacon Baked
      Beans, 153
  Roasted Beet and
      Beet Green Salad
      with Herbs, Goat
      Cheese, and
      Bacon, 50, *51*
  Water Chestnuts
      Wrapped in
      Bacon, 21
bagels
  Backpack Bagel, 213
  everything, seasoning,
      26, *27*, 31, *31*
baguette
  Crab Toast, 15, *15*, *22*,
      23
  Croutons, *52*, 53, *80*, 81
  Herbed Cheese with
      Crostini and
      Radishes, 30, *30*,
      32, *33*
  Tomato Bruschetta,
      10–11, 18, *19*
bananas
  Banana Coffee
      Smoothie, 200

Coconut Banana Bread,
    214, 215
  Pineapple Green
      Smoothie, 200
  Smoothie Bowls, 201
Basil Zucchini Frittata,
    204
BBQ sauce
  BBQ Potato Chip–
      Crusted Salmon
      with Peach Salsa,
      98, 99
  Surf-and-Turf Skewers
      with Spicy
      Bourbon BBQ
      Sauce, *136*, 137
  Women's Club Chicken
      Legs, 128, *129*
beans. *See also*
    cannellini beans
  Peach, Bourbon, and
      Bacon Baked
      Beans, 153
  Veggie Chili Cornbread
      Pot Pie, *114*, 115–16
beef. *See also* steak
  Animal-Style Burgers,
      110, 111
  Beef Gravy, *90*, 91
  Beef Stroganoff, 92, *93*
  Caramelized Onion
      Burgers, *134*, 135
  Penne Pie, 88, *89*
beets
  Roasted Beet and
      Beet Green Salad
      with Herbs, Goat
      Cheese, and
      Bacon, 50, *51*
bell pepper
  Cheat Sheet Sausage,
      Peppers, and
      Onions with
      Polenta, *122*, 123
  Eggs in Purgatory, 196

Turkey Meatloaf, 96, *97*
Veggie Chili Cornbread
    Pot Pie, *114*, 115–16
berries. *See also*
    blueberries;
    strawberries
  Berry Quinoa Porridge,
      212
  Blackberry Cornbread
      Muffins, 205
  Smoothie Bowls, 201
biscuit dough
  Biscuits, 211
  Molasses Spiced
      Monkey Bread,
      202, 203
Blackberry Cornbread
    Muffins, 205
Bloody Mary Shrimp
    Cocktail "Ceviche"
    with Plantain Chips,
    35, *36–37*
blueberries
  Brioche French Toast
      Casserole, 194, *195*
  Smoothie Bowls, 201
blue cheese
  Blue Cheese Dressing,
      40, *41*
  Blue Cheese–Stuffed
      Dates, 28
  Lobster Cobb, 58, *59*
bourbon
  Iced Peach Bourbon
      Lemonade Tea, 13,
      30, *30*
  Peach, Bourbon, and
      Bacon Baked
      Beans, 153
  Spicy Bourbon BBQ
      Sauce, *136*, 137
breadcrumbs
  Eggplant "Meat" Ball
      Sandwiches, 120,
      121

Spaghetti with Clams,
112, *113*
Turkey Meatloaf, 96, *97*
Breakfast Nachos, 198,
199
Brioche French Toast
Casserole, 194, *195*
broccoli
Broccoli au Gratin, 162,
163
Broccoli Green Curry
Coconut Soup, 67
Soy and Lemon
Roasted Broccoli,
152
brown sugar, 104, *105*
Brown Sugar and
Sriracha Bacon,
197
Molasses Spiced
Monkey Bread,
202, 203
Brussels sprouts
Roasted Brussels
Sprouts with
Fresno Chile,
Capers, and
Parmesan, *148*, 149
Shaved Brussels
Sprouts Salad, *44*,
45
burgers
Animal-Style Burgers,
110, 111
Caramelized Onion
Burgers, *134*, 135
butter
Cilantro Honey Butter,
114, 115–16
Herb Butter, 143
buttermilk, 211
Blackberry Cornbread
Muffins, 205
Spicy Buttermilk
Grilled Chicken,
84, 85

butternut squash
Harissa Butternut
Squash Soup, 72
Red Curry Lentil and
Squash Stew, 65
Veggie Chili Cornbread
Pot Pie, *114*, 115–16

———

cabbage
Kale Slaw, *144*, 145
Purple Cauliflower
and Red Cabbage
Salad, *56*, 57
cake mix
Cannoli Trifle, 183
Mango Dump Cake, 182
cannellini beans
Cannellini and Escarole
Soup, *70*, 71
Pork Chops with White
Beans, Fennel, and
Onions, *94*, 95
White Chicken Chili, 73
Cannoli Trifle, 183
capers, *148*, 149
Caramelized Onion
Burgers, *134*, 135
carrots, 74, 75, *118*, 119
Chipotle Carrot Soup,
66
Kale Slaw, *144*, 145
Miso-Carrot-Ginger
Dressing, 61
Roasted Carrots and
Red Leaf Lettuce
Salad with Ranch
Dressing, *48*, 49
cauliflower
Creamy Parmesan
Cauliflower Soup,
68, *69*
Mushroom and Pea
Cauliflower
"Risotto," 150
Purple Cauliflower
and Red Cabbage
Salad, *56*, 57

celery, 74, 75
Celery with Cream
Cheese and
Everything Bagel
Seasoning, 26, *27*,
31, *31*
ceviche, 35, *36–37*
Chard with Almonds and
Raisins, 165
Cheat Sheet Sausage,
Peppers, and Onions
with Polenta, *122*,
123
cheddar, 48, 49
Breakfast Nachos, 198,
199
Broccoli au Gratin, 162,
163
cheese. *See also* blue
cheese; cheddar;
cream cheese; goat
cheese; mozzarella;
Parmesan;
provolone; ricotta
American, *110*, 111
feta, 46, *47*
Gruyère, 108, *109*, *134*,
135
Manchego, 44, 45
pecorino, 124, *125*
cherries, dried, 48, 49
cherry ice cream, 171
chicken
Classic Chicken Noodle
Soup, 74, 75
Grilled Farmers'
Market "Paella,"
138, *139*
Quick Chicken Cutlet
Saltimbocca, 100,
101
Roasted Chicken with
Croutons, *80*, 81
Spicy Buttermilk
Grilled Chicken,
84, 85

Sticky Soy-Ginger-
Garlic Chicken
Thighs, 104, *105*
White Chicken Chili, 73
Women's Club Chicken
Legs, 128, *129*
chickpeas
Pumpkin Hummus, 24,
31, *31*
chiles
Breakfast Nachos, 198,
199
Chipotle Carrot Soup,
66
Eggs in Purgatory, 196
Peach Salsa, 98, 99
Roasted Brussels
Sprouts with
Fresno Chile,
Capers, and
Parmesan, *148*, 149
White Chicken Chili, 73
chili, *114*, 115–16
Chipotle Carrot Soup, 66
chives, 40, *41*
Simple Scrambled Eggs
with Chives, 208
chocolate, 183
Banana Coffee
Smoothie, 200
Chocolate Cherry Ice
Cream Bonbons,
171
Chocolate Croissant
Bread Pudding, 175
Chocolate Pudding, 189
Grandma's Whoopie
Pies, *178*, 179
Miso Chocolate Chunk
Cookies, 180, *181*
Mocha Swirl Ice Cream,
176
cilantro, 98, 99
Cilantro Honey Butter,
114, 115–16
clams
Spaghetti with Clams,
112, *113*

Classic Chicken Noodle
Soup, 74, 75
Cocchi Americano, 16,
31, *31*
cocoa. *See* chocolate
coconut flakes, 182
Coconut Banana Bread,
214, 215
Mom's Granola, 209
coconut milk
Broccoli Green Curry
Coconut Soup, 67
Red Curry Lentil and
Squash Stew, 65
coffee
Affogato, 186, *187*
Banana Coffee
Smoothie, 200
Mocha Swirl Ice Cream,
176
condensed milk
Mocha Swirl Ice Cream,
176
Strawberry Ice Cream,
177
cookies
gingersnap, 170
Grandma's Whoopie
Pies, *178*, 179
Miso Chocolate Chunk
Cookies, 180, *181*
corn
Blackberry Cornbread
Muffins, 205
Crunchy Ranch Corn
on the Cob, 158,
159
Grilled Farmers'
Market "Paella,"
138, *139*
Pesto Farro with
Smoked
Mozzarella,
Arugula, Corn, and
Tomatoes, 54, *55*
cornbread
Blackberry Cornbread
Muffins, 205

Cornbread, *114*, 115–16
Cornbread Dressing
with Herb Butter,
143
Cosmo Americano, 16,
31, *31*
cottage cheese, 170
Crab Toast, 15, *15*, *22*, 23
crackers, 29, 162, *163*
cranberry juice
Cosmo Americano, 16,
31, *31*
cream, 172, *173. See also*
ice cream
Cannoli Trifle, 183
Chocolate Croissant
Bread Pudding, 175
Creamed Spinach, 157
Iron Skillet Lemon
Poppyseed Soufflé,
168, *169*
cream cheese
Celery with Cream
Cheese and
Everything Bagel
Seasoning, 26, *27*,
31, *31*
Creamy Spinach
Artichoke Pasta,
78, *79*
Herbed Cheese with
Crostini and
Radishes, 30, *30*,
32, *33*
Hot Roasted Eggplant
Dip, 34
No-Bake Peanut Butter
Cheesecake, 172,
173
Pumpkin Cheesecake,
170
Creamy Parmesan
Cauliflower Soup,
68, *69*
Crispy Artichoke Hearts,
29
croissants, *174*

Chocolate Croissant
Bread Pudding, 175
Croque Monsieur, 108,
109
Croutons, *52*, 53, *80*, 81
Crunchy Ranch Corn on
the Cob, 158, *159*
cucumbers, 54, *55*, 61
curry
Broccoli Green Curry
Coconut Soup, 67
Grilled Red Curry
Lamb Chops, *130*,
131
Red Curry Lentil and
Squash Stew, 65
Roasted Red Curry
Acorn Squash, 161

———

dates
Blue Cheese–Stuffed
Dates, 28
Shaved Brussels
Sprouts Salad, *44*,
45
Dijon Vinaigrette, 50, *51*
dressings. *See also*
Ranch Dressing
Blue Cheese Dressing,
40, *41*
Creamy Feta Dressing,
46, *47*
French, 128, *129*
House Dressing, 50, *51*
Miso-Carrot-Ginger
Dressing, 61
Poppyseed Dressing,
56, 57
Drop Biscuits, 211

———

Easy Cast-Iron Skillet
Pizza, *126*, 127
eggplant
Eggplant "Meat" Ball
Sandwiches, 120,
121

Grilled Eggplant with
Lemon, Tahini, and
Mint, 160
Hot Roasted Eggplant
Dip, 34
eggs
Basil Zucchini Frittata,
204
Breakfast Nachos, 198,
199
Brioche French Toast
Casserole, 194, *195*
Eggs in Purgatory, 196
Iron Skillet Lemon
Poppyseed Soufflé,
168, *169*
Lemon Caper Deviled
Eggs, *10*, 20
Lobster Cobb, 58, *59*
Simple Scrambled Eggs
with Chives, 208
6, 8, 10 Boiled Eggs, 197
escarole
Cannellini and Escarole
Soup, *70*, 71

———

farro
Pesto Farro with
Smoked
Mozzarella,
Arugula, Corn, and
Tomatoes, 54, *55*
fennel bulb
Arugula, Fennel, and
Citrus Salad, 43
Pork Chops with White
Beans, Fennel, and
Onions, *94*, 95
feta
Greek Salad with
Creamy Feta
Dressing, 46, *47*
Fig and Pepita Goat
Cheese Log, 14, *14*,
25
fish sauce, 104, *105*

Fluffy Pancakes, 206, *207*
Fondant Potatoes, 146, *147*
French dressing, 128, *129*
fudge, 176

———

garlic
  Sticky Soy-Ginger-Garlic Chicken Thighs, 104, *105*
ginger
  Miso-Carrot-Ginger Dressing, 61
  Sticky Soy-Ginger-Garlic Chicken Thighs, 104, *105*
ginger beer
  Mango Mexican Mule, 16
goat cheese
  Fig and Pepita Goat Cheese Log, 14, *14*, 25
  Herbed Cheese with Crostini and Radishes, 30, *30*, 32, *33*
  Roasted Beet and Beet Green Salad with Herbs, Goat Cheese, and Bacon, 50, *51*
  Grandma's Whoopie Pies, *178*, 179
granola
  Bagel, Backpack, 213
  Mom's Granola, 209
  Greek Salad with Creamy Feta Dressing, 46, *47*
Grilled Eggplant with Lemon, Tahini, and Mint, 160
Grilled Farmers' Market "Paella," 138, *139*

Grilled Red Curry Lamb Chops, *130*, 131
Grilled Sweet Potato and Arugula Salad, 42
Grilled Tuna Salad with Miso-Carrot-Ginger Dressing, 61

———

ham
  Apricot-Glazed Ham, 117
  Croque Monsieur, 108, *109*
Harissa Butternut Squash Soup, 72
herbs
  Herb Butter, 143
  Herbed Cheese with Crostini and Radishes, 30, *30*, 32, *33*
  Herbed Oven Fries, 156
  Roasted Beet and Beet Green Salad with Herbs, Goat Cheese, and Bacon, 50, *51*
hoisin sauce
  Ryan's Ribs—Hoisin Style, 86, *87*
honey
  Cilantro Honey Butter, *114*, 115–16
  Hot Roasted Eggplant Dip, 34
hot sauce
  Brown Sugar and Sriracha Bacon, 197
  Spicy Buttermilk Grilled Chicken, *84*, 85
  Surf-and-Turf Skewers with Spicy Bourbon BBQ Sauce, *136*, 137
  House Dressing, 50, *51*

Hummus, Pumpkin, 24, 31, *31*

———

Iceberg Disk Salad, 40, *41*
ice cream
  Affogato, 186, *187*
  Chocolate Cherry Ice Cream Bonbons, 171
  Mocha Swirl Ice Cream, 176
  Strawberry Ice Cream, 177
  Iced Peach Bourbon Lemonade Tea, 13, 30, *30*
  Iron Skillet Lemon Poppyseed Soufflé, 168, *169*

———

jalapeños. *See* chiles

———

Kalamatas, 46, *47*
kale, 50, *51*
  Kale Slaw, *144*, 145
  Spicy Kale Caesar with Crispy Onions, Almonds, Avocado, and Croutons, *52*, 53
ketchup
  Peach, Bourbon, and Bacon Baked Beans, 153
  Special Sauce, *110*, 111
  Turkey Meatloaf, 96, *97*

———

lamb chops
  Grilled Red Curry Lamb Chops, *130*, 131

lemon
  Grilled Eggplant with Lemon, Tahini, and Mint, 160
  Iron Skillet Lemon Poppyseed Soufflé, 168, *169*
  Lemon Caper Deviled Eggs, *10*, 20
  Lemon Pasta, 132, *133*
  Soy and Lemon Roasted Broccoli, 152
lemonade
  Iced Peach Bourbon Lemonade Tea, 13, 30, *30*
lemon sorbet
  Affogato, 186, *187*
  Sgroppino, 14, *14*, 17
lentils
  Red Curry Lentil and Squash Stew, 65
lettuce/salad greens
  Bistro Salad, *80*, 81
  Greek Salad with Creamy Feta Dressing, 46, *47*
  Grilled Tuna Salad with Miso-Carrot-Ginger Dressing, 61
  Iceberg Disk Salad, 40, *41*
  Lobster Cobb, 58, *59*
  Roasted Carrots and Red Leaf Lettuce Salad with Ranch Dressing, 48, 49
Lillet Fizz, 13, 15, *15*
Lobster Cobb, 58, *59*

———

mango
  Mango Dump Cake, 182
  Mango Mexican Mule, 16
  Smoothie Bowls, 201

Maple-Sage Roasted
    Turkey in 8 Pieces,
    106, 107
marinara sauce
    Eggplant "Meat" Ball
        Sandwiches, 120,
        121
    Eggs in Purgatory, 196
    Penne Pie, 88, *89*
marshmallow crème
    Grandma's Whoopie
        Pies, *178*, 179
mayonnaise
    Blue Cheese Dressing,
        40, *41*
    Hot Roasted Eggplant
        Dip, 34
    Lemon Caper Deviled
        Eggs, *10*, 20
    Special Sauce, *110*, 111
Meatloaf, Turkey, 96, *97*
milk. *See also*
    buttermilk;
    condensed milk;
    cream
    Brioche French Toast
        Casserole, 194, *195*
    Chocolate Pudding, 189
mint
    Grilled Eggplant with
        Lemon, Tahini, and
        Mint, 160
    Pineapple Green
        Smoothie, 200
miso
    Miso-Carrot-Ginger
        Dressing, 61
    Miso Chocolate Chunk
        Cookies, 180, *181*
    Miso Twice-Baked
        Japanese Sweet
        Potatoes, 164
    Mocha Swirl Ice Cream,
        176
    Molasses Spiced Monkey
        Bread, *202*, 203
    Mom's Granola, 209

mozzarella
    Creamy Spinach
        Artichoke Pasta,
        78, *79*
    Easy Cast-Iron Skillet
        Pizza, *126*, 127
    Hot Roasted Eggplant
        Dip, 34
    Penne Pie, 88, *89*
    Pesto Farro with
        Smoked
        Mozzarella,
        Arugula, Corn, and
        Tomatoes, 54, *55*
mushrooms
    Beef Stroganoff, 92, *93*
    Broccoli au Gratin, 162,
        163
    Eggplant "Meat" Ball
        Sandwiches, 120,
        121
    Mushroom and Pea
        Cauliflower
        "Risotto," 150
    Mushroom Bolognese
        with Rigatoni, *118*,
        119

———

No-Bake Peanut Butter
    Cheesecake, 172, *173*
noodles. *See also* pasta
    Beef Stroganoff, 92, *93*
    Classic Chicken Noodle
        Soup, 74, 75

———

oats
    Mom's Granola, 209
    Stone Fruit Crisp, 190,
        191
    Oil and Vinegar Herbed
        Potato Salad, 62, *63*
olives, 46, *47*
onions
    Caramelized Onion
        Burgers, *134*, 135

Cheat Sheet Sausage,
    Peppers, and
    Onions with
    Polenta, *122*, 123
Pork Chops with White
    Beans, Fennel, and
    Onions, *94*, 95
Spicy Kale Caesar with
    Crispy Onions,
    Almonds, Avocado,
    and Croutons, *52*,
    53
orange liqueur, 183
oranges, 43, *136*, 137

———

Pancakes, 206, *207*
Parmesan, 34, 78, *79*,
    204
    Creamy Parmesan
        Cauliflower Soup,
        68, *69*
    Eggplant "Meat" Ball
        Sandwiches, 120,
        121
    Lemon Pasta, 132, *133*
    Penne Pie, 88, *89*
    Roasted Brussels
        Sprouts with
        Fresno Chile,
        Capers, and
        Parmesan, *148*, 149
    Spaghetti with
        Zucchini, 124, *125*
pasta
    Creamy Spinach
        Artichoke Pasta,
        78, *79*
    Lemon Pasta, 132, *133*
    Mushroom Bolognese
        with Rigatoni, *118*,
        119
    Penne Pie, 88, *89*
    Spaghetti with Clams,
        112, *113*
    Spaghetti with
        Zucchini, 124, *125*

peaches
    Peach, Bourbon, and
        Bacon Baked
        Beans, 153
    Peach Salsa, 98, *99*
    Stone Fruit Crisp, 190,
        191
peach schnapps, 13, 30,
    30
peanut butter
    Bagel, Backpack, 213
    No-Bake Peanut Butter
        Cheesecake, 172,
        173
peas
    Mushroom and Pea
        Cauliflower
        "Risotto," 150
    Penne Pie, 88, *89*
pepitas
    Fig and Pepita Goat
        Cheese Log, 14,
        14, 25
pepperoncini, 46, *47*
Pesto Farro with
    Smoked Mozzarella,
    Arugula, Corn, and
    Tomatoes, 54, *55*
pineapple
    Pineapple Green
        Smoothie, 200
    Smoothie Bowls, 201
pistachios, 50, *51*
    Cannoli Trifle, 183
    Sweet Potatoes with
        Cumin Yogurt,
        Pomegranates, and
        Pistachios, 154, *155*
pizza
    Easy Cast-Iron Skillet
        Pizza, *126*, 127
plantain chips, 35, *36–37*
plums, 190, *191*
polenta
    Cheat Sheet Sausage,
        Peppers, and
        Onions with
        Polenta, *122*, 123

pomegranate, 50, *51*
  Arugula, Fennel, and
    Citrus Salad, 43
  Sweet Potatoes with
    Cumin Yogurt,
    Pomegranates, and
    Pistachios, 154, *155*
poppyseeds
  Iron Skillet Lemon
    Poppyseed Soufflé,
    168, *169*
  Poppyseed Dressing,
    56, 57
Pork Chops with White
    Beans, Fennel, and
    Onions, *94*, 95
Porterhouse Steak in an
    Iron Skillet, 82, *83*
potato chips
  BBQ Potato Chip–
    Crusted Salmon
    with Peach Salsa,
    98, 99
potatoes
  Fondant Potatoes, 146,
    147
  Herbed Oven Fries, 156
  Oil and Vinegar Herbed
    Potato Salad, 62,
    63
  Simple Mashed
    Potatoes, 142
Prime Rib with Beef
    Gravy, *90*, 91
prosciutto
  Prosciutto Crisps, 14,
    14, 28
  Quick Chicken Cutlet
    Saltimbocca, 100,
    101
prosecco
  Amalfi Spritz, 12, 15, *15*
  Sgroppino, 14, *14*, 17
provolone
  Eggplant "Meat" Ball
    Sandwiches, 120,
    121

Quick Chicken Cutlet
    Saltimbocca, 100,
    101
pumpkin
  Pumpkin Cheesecake,
    170
  Pumpkin Hummus, 24,
    31, *31*
pumpkin seeds
  Fig and Pepita Goat
    Cheese Log, 14,
    14, 25
  Mom's Granola, 209
Purple Cauliflower and
    Red Cabbage Salad,
    56, 57

———

Quick Chicken Cutlet
    Saltimbocca, 100,
    101
quinoa
  Berry Quinoa Porridge,
    212

———

radishes
  Herbed Cheese with
    Crostini and
    Radishes, 30, *30*,
    32, *33*
raisins, 165
Ranch Dressing
  Crunchy Ranch Corn
    on the Cob, 158,
    159
  recipe, *48*, 49
Red Curry Lentil and
    Squash Stew, 65
ribs
  Ryan's Ribs—Hoisin
    Style, 86, *87*
rice
  Grilled Farmers'
    Market "Paella,"
    138, *139*
ricotta
  Cannoli Trifle, 183

Penne Pie, 88, *89*
Roasted Beet and Beet
    Green Salad with
    Herbs, Goat Cheese,
    and Bacon, 50, *51*
Roasted Brussels
    Sprouts with Fresno
    Chile, Capers, and
    Parmesan, *148*, 149
Roasted Carrots and
    Red Leaf Lettuce
    Salad with Ranch
    Dressing, *48*, 49
Roasted Chicken with
    Croutons, *80*, 81
Roasted Red Curry
    Acorn Squash, 161
Ryan's Ribs—Hoisin
    Style, 86, *87*

———

sage, 100, *101*
  Maple-Sage Roasted
    Turkey in 8 Pieces,
    106, 107
salmon
  BBQ Potato Chip–
    Crusted Salmon
    with Peach Salsa,
    98, 99
salsa
  Veggie Chili Cornbread
    Pot Pie, *114*, 115–16
  White Chicken Chili, 73
sandwiches
  Croque Monsieur, 108,
    109
  Eggplant "Meat" Ball
    Sandwiches, 120,
    121
sausage
  Breakfast Nachos, 198,
    199
  Cheat Sheet Sausage,
    Peppers, and
    Onions with
    Polenta, *122*, 123

Grilled Farmers'
    Market "Paella,"
    138, *139*
Sgroppino, 14, *14*, 17
Shaved Brussels Sprouts
    Salad, *44*, 45
sherry, 92, *93*
shrimp
  Bloody Mary Shrimp
    Cocktail "Ceviche"
    with Plantain
    Chips, 35, *36–37*
  Skillet Broiled Shrimp,
    102, 103
  Surf-and-Turf Skewers
    with Spicy
    Bourbon BBQ
    Sauce, *136*, 137
Simple Mashed
    Potatoes, 142
Simple Scrambled Eggs
    with Chives, 208
6, 8, 10 Boiled Eggs, 197
Skillet Broiled Shrimp,
    102, 103
smoothies
  Banana Coffee
    Smoothie, 200
  Pineapple Green
    Smoothie, 200
  Smoothie Bowls, 201
sour cream, 92, *93*
soy sauce
  Soy and Lemon
    Roasted Broccoli,
    152
  Sticky Soy-Ginger-
    Garlic Chicken
    Thighs, 104, *105*
Spaghetti with Clams,
    112, *113*
Spaghetti with Zucchini,
    124, *125*
Special Sauce, *110*, 111
Spicy Buttermilk Grilled
    Chicken, *84*, 85

Spicy Kale Caesar with
 Crispy Onions
 Almonds, Avocado,
 and Croutons, *52*, 53
spinach, 65
 Creamed Spinach, 157
 Creamy Spinach
  Artichoke Pasta,
  78, *79*
 Pineapple Green
  Smoothie, 200
squash, summer,
 138, *139. See also*
 zucchini
squash, winter. *See also*
 butternut squash
 Roasted Red Curry
  Acorn Squash, 161
Sriracha. *See* hot sauce
steak
 Porterhouse Steak in
  an Iron Skillet,
  82, *83*
 Surf-and-Turf Skewers
  with Spicy
  Bourbon BBQ
  Sauce, *136*, 137
Sticky Soy-Ginger-Garlic
 Chicken Thighs,
 104, *105*
Stone Fruit Crisp, 190,
 191
strawberries
 Smoothie Bowls, 201
 Strawberry Ice Cream,
  177
sunflower seeds, *48*, 49,
 209
Surf-and-Turf Skewers
 with Spicy Bourbon
 BBQ Sauce, *136*, 137
sweet potatoes
 Breakfast Nachos, 198,
  199
 Grilled Sweet Potato
  and Arugula Salad,
  42

Miso Twice-Baked
 Japanese Sweet
 Potatoes, 164
Sweet Potatoes with
 Cumin Yogurt,
 Pomegranates, and
 Pistachios, 154, *155*
sweet relish, *110*, 111
Swiss Chard with
 Almonds and
 Raisins, 165

———

tahini
 Grilled Eggplant with
  Lemon, Tahini, and
  Mint, 160
 Pumpkin Hummus, 24,
  31, *31*
tea, 13, 30, *30*
tequila
 Mango Mexican Mule,
  16
 Tequila and Tonic, 12
tomatoes, canned, *118*,
 119
 Red Curry Lentil and
  Squash Stew, 65
 Veggie Chili Cornbread
  Pot Pie, *114*, 115–16
tomatoes, cherry/grape
 Greek Salad with
  Creamy Feta
  Dressing, 46, *47*
 Grilled Farmers'
  Market "Paella,"
  138, *139*
 Iceberg Disk Salad,
  40, *41*
 Lobster Cobb, 58, *59*
 Pesto Farro with
  Smoked
  Mozzarella,
  Arugula, Corn, and
  Tomatoes, 54, *55*
 Tomato Bruschetta,
  10–11, 18, *19*

Tuna Salad with Miso-
 Carrot-Ginger
 Dressing, Grilled, 61
turkey
 Maple-Sage Roasted
  Turkey in 8 Pieces,
  106, 107
 Turkey Meatloaf, 96, *97*

———

Veggie Chili Cornbread
 Pot Pie, *114*, 115–16
vodka
 Cosmo Americano, 16,
  31, *31*
 Sgroppino, 14, *14*, 17

———

Water Chestnuts
 Wrapped in Bacon,
 21
White Chicken Chili, 73
Women's Club Chicken
 Legs, 128, *129*

———

yogurt, *126*, 127
 Kale Slaw, *144*, 145
 Sweet Potatoes with
  Cumin Yogurt,
  Pomegranates, and
  Pistachios, 154, *155*

———

zucchini
 Basil Zucchini Frittata,
  204
 Grilled Farmers'
  Market "Paella,"
  138, *139*
 Spaghetti with
  Zucchini, 124, *125*

Editor: Holly Dolce
Designer: Deb Wood
Production Manager: Anet Sirna-Bruder

Library of Congress Control Number: 2020944144

ISBN: 978-1-4197-4853-0
eISBN: 978-1-64700-065-3

Abrams books are available at special discounts when
purchased in quantity for premiums and promotions as
well as fundraising or educational use. Special editions
can also be created to specification. For details, contact
specialsales@abramsbooks.com or the address below.

Abrams® is a registered trademark of
Harry N. Abrams, Inc.

ABRAMS
The Art of Books

195 Broadway
New York, NY 10007
abramsbooks.com